Happy 22 J!.
To the only person
I know who tries to
be Irish! Just always
remember I'll always be mom!
All my luck as you get
older - Always,
Melissa

The Irish American PUB QUIZ

Liam McAtasney

Produced by the Philip Lief Group Inc.

MJF BOOKS
NEW YORK

Published by MJF Books
Fine Communications
Two Lincoln Square
60 West 66th Street
New York, NY 10023

Irish American Pub Quiz
LC Control Number 00-132856
ISBN 1-56731-404-X

Copyright © 1999 by Liam McAtasney and the Philip Lief Group Inc.

This edition published by arrangement with Andrews McMeel Publishing.
Designed and composed by Kelly & Company, Lee's Summit, Missouri

Manufactured in the United States of America on acid-free paper

MJF Books and the MJF colophon are trademarks of Fine Creative Media,
Inc.

10   9   8   7   6   5   4   3   2   1

To Annie and Sally

Contents

Acknowledgments

I would like to thank to all the people who have given me ideas for this book and in particular everyone who has helped make this book a reality: Finbarr Fleming, Noel McAtasney, Adrian "Danny Boy" McAlinden, Carol Farrand, Martin "The Celt" Donnelly, and John Boisson.

Irish Promotions
2265 Larkin Street, Ste. 19
San Francisco, CA 94109-1956
Liam @ (415) 931-1855
.

Preface

Cultural anthropologists are still debating the precise origins of today's hugely popular pub quiz, a "live" trivia quiz show administered by a "quizmaster" to teams of bar goers everywhere. Traditionally scheduled for an "off" night (usually Sunday through Thursday), the pub quiz is a revenue boon for bar owners and provides lively entertainment in a friendly, social atmosphere for anyone old enough to go to a bar.

Though the truth is still shrouded in a barroom haze, most likely the pub quiz evolved in Britain and Ireland in the early days of television. Pubs, of course, have always been places to drink, socialize, and relax. But in the 1940s, many pubs had another draw: Unlike most homes, the pubs had television. Televised game shows in particular drew the imbibers' great attention. Pub regulars often called out answers to game show questions before the studio contestants did, prompting fellow pub goers to shout, "Why don't you go on that show?" to the most knowledgeable bar "contestants."

The friendly rivalry, lighthearted banter, and increased bar business attributable to the television quiz shows inspired pub owners to offer live quiz shows as a regular feature on their pub entertainment calendars. At one point, as many as five hundred teams competed in weekly interpub matches in Lancashire County, England. To this day live quiz shows enjoy immense popularity throughout Britain and Ireland.

In the United States, pub quiz shows thrive in San Francisco, Boston, New York, and other cities popular with those of Anglo-Irish descent. Bars in these cities host weekly pub trivia quiz shows, packing the house with trivia fans eager to show their prowess. Teams formed of friends, coworkers, family (and even the occasional stranger at the bar) battle each other over rounds of questions fired at them by the host or pub quizmaster.

More Americans will be able to enjoy the fun and excitement of the pub quiz at their favorite local bar once bar owners realize its money-making potential. Besides offering a great way to meet new people (including members of the opposite sex!), the pub quiz invites participants to flex their trivia muscles and perhaps even win a prize or two.

The Brainstormer Pub Quiz questions in this book cover a broad range of Irish and Irish American trivia. Brainstormer Pub Quiz provides complete Pub Trivia Quiz Show kits (including prizes) that appeal universally to bars, clubs, and corporations and radio and print media. To host a Brainstormer Pub Quiz at your bar, office, club, or private party, or to receive more information, please call Brainstormer Pub Quiz toll free at (877) PUB-QUIZ (782-7849), or check out our Web site at www.brainstormer.com or www.brainstormerpubquiz.com, where you will also find contests and prizes galore.

Meanwhile, get your brain in gear, get your Irish up, and enjoy the challenge!

Cheers!
Liam McAtasney

ONE
Ireland Through the Ages: Irish History

1. Protestant colonists and the British government imposed a vast system of social, political, and economic control upon Catholics in the years following the Battle of the Boyne. What is the term used to describe this imposition?

2. Catholic farmers were required to pay one-tenth of their income/harvest to the Protestant Church of Ireland. What was the payment called?

3. What series of laws had a provision that forbade Catholics from possessing a horse valued at more than five pounds?

4. This group, which held its first meeting on October 18, 1791, envisioned an independent Irish republic offering equal citizenship to both Protestants and Catholics.

5. The Rebellion of 1798 began at a village called Boolabogue and ended with a crushing British victory at this place.

6. In what century were the traditional province boundaries of Ireland set?

> **a.** sixteenth
> **b.** seventeenth
> **c.** eighteenth

7. Who was the Irish missionary who supposedly sailed west across the Atlantic and discovered America long before the Vikings or Columbus?

8. This was the worst year of the famine in Ireland, when hundreds of thousands perished from hunger and disease.

9. Who was the director of the British government's Irish relief measures who rejected all proposals for government-assisted emigration from Ireland during the famine?

10. What British newspaper declared that the famine in Ireland was "a great blessing"?

11. Approximately how many people left Ireland between 1801 and 1900?

> **a.** 4 million
> **b.** 6 million
> **c.** 8 million

12. In 1997 who became the first Irish Republican leader to enter Downing Street for talks with a British prime minister since Michael Collins did so in 1921?

13. Identify the speaker of this quote: "My heart is very sore because I know that I have broken my poor mother's heart. . . ."

14. From the steps of the General Post Office (on what is now O'Connell Street in Dublin), what document did Padraig Pearse read on Easter Monday, April 24, 1916?

15. Formed in County Armagh in the last years of the eighteenth century, this organization is estimated to have between forty thousand and fifty thousand members on the island of Ireland. Name it.

16. In June of 1919 the first successful nonstop transatlantic flight, piloted by British pilots Alcock and Brown, touched down near what town in County Galway?

17. Name the two women who founded the "Peace People" movement and won the 1976 Nobel Peace Prize for their work in mobilizing the general public for peace.

18. Two years earlier, another Irish figure—a onetime IRA leader and former United Nations assistant secretary general—was awarded the prize for his work as an international jurist and diplomat. Name him.

19. How did Saint Patrick first arrive in Ireland?

20. In what century is Saint Patrick credited with converting the Irish to Christianity?

> **a.** fifth
> **b.** sixth
> **c.** seventh

21. This great-grandson of Queen Victoria was killed by the IRA at Mullaghmore in Ireland in 1979. Name him.

22. What was the ancient capital of Ireland?

23. According to a book published in 1998, what British prime minister had considered repartition, the concept that the border could be redrawn and that Irish nationalists be forcefully repatriated to the Republic of Ireland?

24. He was a founder of the Credit Union movement in Ireland in the late 1960s, a financial system that helped liberate many who were caught in the poverty trap. Name him.

25. Name the statesman and lawyer, son of Maud Gonne, who died in 1988.

26. What English king opened the first Northern Ireland Parliament in Belfast on June 7, 1921?

27. Who was the commander in chief of the Dublin forces during the 1916 Easter Rising?

28. A statue of this British military figure was blown up in Dublin in 1966. Name him.

29. Who was perhaps Ireland's most famous visitor in 1979?

30. Who led thousands of Unionists to sign the Ulster Solemn League and Covenant on September 28, 1912, opposing the Home Rule bill and reaffirming Protestant support for the union with Britain?

31. What British member of Parliament, shadow Northern Ireland secretary (the member of the opposition party who would become secretary of Northern Ireland if his party assumed power), was killed by a bomb as he drove from the House of Commons car park in 1979?

32. A British force of about six thousand men was shipped to Ireland during the Irish War of Independence. They soon acquired a nickname due to the mismatching colors of their uniforms. Who were they?

33. Who invaded Ireland around 1169?

34. How many civilians were killed as a result of British army actions during an anti-internment march in Derry in 1972?

35. In 1998 it was announced by the Irish government that the original *Asgard*—used by Erskine Childers to ship rifles in 1914—was to be refurbished. At what Irish port did the *Asgard* arrive in the 1914 gun-running incident?

36. What happened to Joseph Plunkett, one of the leaders of the 1916 Easter Rising, about five hours before he was executed?

37. His victory over James II is celebrated each year by Orangemen around the world. Name him.

38. In what year did Ireland join NATO?

39. Who, along with Michael Collins, arranged Eamon DeValera's escape from Lincoln jail in 1919?

40. By the second half of the seventeenth century, and even more during the eighteenth century, this developed into Ireland's greatest industry. What was it?

41. In the 1990s what Irish politician became associated with the phrase "spilling our sweat and not our blood"?

42. In 1979 the French tanker *Betelgeuse* exploded in Bantry Bay, resulting in fifty deaths, making it the worst industrial disaster in Ireland. On what island did the disaster occur?

Irish History 7

Irish Folklore and Mythology

43. What is the usual occupation of the leprechaun of Irish legend?

44. What is said to be bestowed on those who kiss the Blarney stone?

45. In Irish mythology, who ate the "salmon of knowledge"?

46. What was the name of Finn McCool's dog?

47. In mythology, who was Oisin's son?

48. Who was known as the "Hound of Ulster"?

49. According to Irish myth, how many sons did Cuchulainn have?

50. The Romans had Neptune, and the Greeks had Poseidon. Who is the Celtic equivalent of these gods of the sea?

51. Her wail pierces the night, its notes rising and falling like the waves of the sea, always announcing a mortal's death. Who is she?

52. It was said that this mythical warrior queen could outdrink and outfight all of her warriors. No king of Connaught could rule without her as queen, and her sexual union with these favored men created heroes and rulers alike. Who was she?

53. According to legend, she teases men with her beauty, and her singing (or siren song) is described as irresistible. As she lounges upon the rocks, she attempts to attract fishermen to her; but if they come too close, she dives into the sea, laughing at them. Who is she?

54. What name is given to the gentle creatures who are seals by day but men and women by night?

55. Folk legends associated with this "gray rocky place" say its holy wells can cure bad vision and that its caves are home to ghostly horsemen. It is also reputed that mysterious lakes appear and disappear there, taking with them maidens who have been turned into swans. What is this place?

56. In more recent times Irish folklore has led to such Hallow Eve practices as lighting a good fire for these spirits. People avoided taking shortcuts across beaches, fields, or cliffs for fear they would lead them astray. They love milk and honey and drink flower nectar as their wine. What are they?

57. This group comprises warriors who protected Erin from outside marauders. They also acted as mediators when conflicts arose between the five lesser kingdoms of Erin, namely Ulster, Munster, Connaught, Leinster, and Meath. What is the name of this group?

TWO
From Mizen Head to Malin Head: Irish Geography

58. Ireland is divided into how many counties?

59. Alphabetically, what Irish county comes first?

60. And what county comes last?

61. St. George's Channel separates Ireland and what country?

62. What is Ireland's longest river?

63. What is the highest point in Ireland?

64. What country is Ireland's nearest neighbor?

65. What Irish city is served by Aldergrove Airport?

66. In what Irish county is the Hill of Tara?

67. What river separates the town of Strabane from County Donegal?

68. What mountain range is celebrated in the famous ballad by Percy French?

69. Which is the highest peak in that mountain range?

70. What county has the shortest coastline?

71. What Irish city is overlooked by Black Mountain?

72. In what county might you visit the Giant's Causeway?

Irish Waterways

For each of the following towns and cities, name the waterway that runs through or by it. (Choices: River Blackwater, River Lagan, River Liffey, River Lee, Ulster Canal, River Nore, River Boyne, River Foyle, River Suir, River Bann)

73. Cork

74. Dublin

75. Derry

76. Belfast

77. Slane

78. Clones

79. Kilkenny

80. Mallow

81. Portadown

82. Waterford

🍀 🍀 🍀

83. What is the second longest river in Ireland?

84. In what county is Ashford Castle?

85. What county in Munster lies west of the River Shannon?

86. At 2,466 feet, the peak of this mountain is the highest point in County Donegal. Name the mountain.

87. If you land at Shannon Airport, what county are you in?

88. If you arrive at Knock International Airport, what county are you in?

89. Kilronan is the largest town on what group of islands?

90. How many main islands are in this group of islands?

91. Name them.

92. In what county is Monasterboice?

93. What is Ireland's northernmost county?

94. What mountain in the Macgillicuddy's Reeks is 3,415 feet high?

95. What Irish county is surrounded by Kildare, Laois, Kilkenny, Wexford, and Wicklow?

96. How many Irish counties begin with the letter "M"?

97. Off the coast of what county are the Seven Hogs and Blasket Island?

98. Ireland is divided into how many provinces?

99. Name them.

100. Name the easternmost province.

101. Name the largest lake in Ireland, which is also the largest freshwater lake in the British Isles.

102. Approximately how long is the border that separates Northern Ireland and the Republic of Ireland?

> **a.** 200 miles
> **b.** 250 miles
> **c.** 300 miles
> **d.** 325 miles

103. How many bodies of water surround Ireland?

104. Name them.

105. What mountains, along the northeastern coast of Ireland, are extensions of the Scottish Highlands?

106. This city's walls are eighteen feet high and twenty feet thick and have never been breached. Hence its nickname: "The Maiden City." Name the city.

107. What Irish county contains the coastal towns of Bangor, Donaghadee, Newcastle, and Warrenpoint?

108. Its rich fruit-growing area has earned this county the nickname "the Orchard County."

109. Does the River Liffey flow north, south, east, or west?

110. In what Irish county might you kiss the Blarney stone?

111. St. Patrick's Purgatory is widely recognized as having one of the toughest three-day pilgrimages and penitential exercises anywhere in the world. In the middle of what lake is it located?

112. This area has the largest karstic limestone deposits in Western Europe and is known internationally for both its unique flora and its spectacular archaeology.

113. In what Irish county is it located?

114. Name Ireland's largest island.

115. How many counties are there in the province of Ulster?

Irish Counties

For each of the next ten questions, you will be given three clues to help you determine different Irish counties. For fun, give yourself three points if you correctly guess the county after reading the first clue, two points after the second, and one point after the third (and easiest!) clue.

    116. a. It is situated on an extensive plain. Except for a hilly region in the northeast, the land is low and fertile.

        b. At 317 square miles, it is Ireland's smallest county.

        c. Dundalk is the county town.

117. a. It is part of the province of Munster and had a population of approximately 122,000 in 1991.

b. It is Ireland's westernmost county.

c. Climbing is excellent in this county and includes the highest mountain in Ireland.

118. a. Common last names in this county include McCann, Donnelly, Watson, and Quinn.

b. It borders County Down.

c. Its capital city has been Ireland's ecclesiastical capital for 1,500 years.

119. a. It is famous for its stout.

b. The city center of this county's largest city is built on an island in the river just upstream of the harbor.

c. It contains the second city in the Republic of Ireland.

120. a. Famous sons of this county include the duke of Wellington, Jonathan Swift, and Saint Oliver Plunkett.

b. It was ruled by the kings of pagan and early Christian Ireland.

c. The Battle of the Boyne was fought here.

121. a. Its rivers, including the Cladagh, have claimed many world coarse angling match records.

   b. The Marble Arch Caves are a major attraction in this county.

   c. The pottery factory in this county was established in 1857 and still employs nineteenth-century techniques.

122. a. The northern landscape is dominated by steep-sided, flat-topped limestone hills.

   b. This county's towns include Tubbercurry, Ballymote, and the popular holiday resort Bundoran.

   c. W. B. Yeats is buried here.

123. a. This county is great for angling, golf, mountain walking, and caving, and it has castles, abbeys, and forts to explore.

   b. It is fashioned by the Galtee Mountains, the River Suir, and a lush green landscape.

   c. If you were in Waterford, you wouldn't have "a long way to go" to get here!

124. a. The eastern boundary of this county is formed by the River Shannon and Lough Derg.

   b. Many consider this county to be the musical capital of Ireland. Christy Moore sang, ". . . if it's music you want, you should go [here]."

   c. Its famous Cliffs of Moher rise seven hundred feet above the sea.

125. **a.** It is an inland county with many island-dotted lakes.

   b. This county borders Offaly to the southeast across the River Shannon.

   c. The Famine Museum at Strokestown is in this county.

126. Which is bigger, Ireland or Iceland?

127. In what Irish county is Slieve Gullion (1,893 feet), the highest point?

128. The northeast of Ireland is characterized by a plateau comprising what kind of rock?

129. What is believed to have separated Ireland from the European mainland?

130. In what Irish county would you visit Dunluce and Carrickfergus Castles?

131. What Irish canal was the first to establish the important principle of water supply to an artificial system and a central high-point reservoir?

132. What street in Dublin was at one time the widest street in Europe?

133. Saint Patrick used to tend sheep on Slemish Mountain, which is in what Irish county?

134. The Japanese Gardens and Maynooth College are in this county, which has a snake on its crest.

135. Approximately how many miles is it from Belfast to Dublin?

> **a.** 75
> **b.** 95
> **c.** 105

136. The Aran Islands lie off the coast of County Clare. Off the coast of what Irish county does Aran Island lie?

137. What is Ireland's second largest lake?

> **a.** Lough Ree
> **b.** Lough Corrib
> **c.** Lough Erne

138. How many counties in Ulster border Lough Neagh?

139. True or false? Ireland is the westernmost country in Europe.

THREE
The Irish Across the Atlantic: Irish America

140. What U.S. state has the most residents claiming Irish ancestry?

141. By what more popular name do we know the western scout and showman William Cody?

142. Who was the first Irish American Catholic ambassador to England?

143. The St. Patrick's Day parade in this southern city attracts the third largest crowd after New York and Boston.

144. What decade of the nineteenth century saw the greatest number of Irish immigrate to the United States?

145. Of all the foreign-born residents of the United States in 1870, approximately what percentage was Irish?

>   **a.** 23 percent
>   **b.** 33 percent
>   **c.** 43 percent

146. In which U.S. state would you find the towns Derry, Londonderry, and Dublin?

147. The island of Ireland covers an area of approximately 32,588 square miles. What U.S. state is closest in size?

148. In his 1996 book, *Sweet Liberty: Travels in Irish America,* Joseph O'Connor tours the United States to visit different towns named "Dublin." How many Dublins did he set out to visit?

> **a.** six
> **b.** nine
> **c.** twelve

149. In which state did the Molly Maguires originate?

150. Numerous lives were lost, many of them Irish, in building this bridge, one of the greatest technical achievements of the nineteenth century. Name this "eighth wonder of the world," which opened in 1883.

151. Archbishop John Hughes is responsible for the building of what American landmark that attracts over three million people each year?

152. Identify the speaker of this quote: "Ask not what your country can do for you—ask what you can do for your country."

153. Approximately how many Americans trace all or part of their ancestry to Irish immigrants?

      a. 25 million
      b. 35 million
      c. 40 million

154. Of what religion were most of the "Scotch-Irish" who came to America from Ulster in the decades before and after the American Revolution?

155. In which year did Ellis Island officially become the entry point for immigrants to the United States?

      a. 1848
      b. 1892
      c. 1906

156. The first immigrant to enter the United States via Ellis Island was a fifteen-year-old Irish girl. What was her name?

157. Identify the speaker of this quote: "I'm in the labor movement, and I speak my own piece."

158. What midwestern city had the highest percentage of Irish-born inhabitants of any city in the United States at the beginning of the twentieth century?

159. What newspaper, founded in 1928, claims to have the largest circulation of any Irish American newspaper?

160. The last time this organization marched through the streets of New York City (July 1871), scores died and more than one hundred were injured in clashes with police and militiamen. Name the organization.

161. According to Kerby Miller and Paul Wagner, authors of *Out of Ireland: The Story of Irish Emigration to America*, how many men and women left Ireland to come to America in the eighteenth, nineteenth, and twentieth centuries?

> **a.** 5 million
> **b.** 7 million
> **c.** 10 million
> **d.** 12 million

162. By 1910 approximately two hundred thousand Irish American men and women were members of which Irish American organization?

163. Name the secret society initiated and directed by James Stephens in the 1860s to oppose British rule in Ireland.

164. What "first" does John McCloskey hold in the United States?

165. In what U.S. state is O'Neill, "the Irish Capital of the West"?

166. What Irish American's wealth was estimated at more than $250 million in 1957?

167. What U.S. state includes the towns of Limerick, Waterford, Waterville, and Belfast?

168. This woman, born of Irish Socialist parents, was known as a feminist and the first woman to head the U.S. Communist Party. She died in Moscow in 1964. Who was she?

169. What is the name of the registered charitable organization with established offices in Dublin and Boston whose mission is to promote the economic development of Ireland through investment in job creation and education?

170. Name the Irish-born U.S. Roman Catholic clergyman and social reformer who was archbishop of St. Paul, Minnesota, from 1888 to 1918.

171. He earned twenty-nine Irish rugby caps before making it to the top in corporate America as chairman of the H. J. Heinz Corporation. Name him.

172. Identify the speaker of this quote: "He didn't even have the satisfaction of being killed for civil rights. . . . It had to be some silly little Communist."

173. What gangster survived the St. Valentine's Day Massacre in 1929 because he was late arriving that day, and eventually died of lung cancer in Leavenworth prison in 1957?

174. Besides being in the top position of Mutual of America, he has played a very big part in contributing to peace in Northern Ireland by using his extensive business contacts to encourage parties on both sides of the conflict to come together. Who is he?

175. This former choirboy turned gangster was raised in the Little Hell district of Chicago and was the leader of a large and powerful gang called the "North Siders." He died under orders from John Torrio. Name him.

176. What American city has a section called the "Irish Channel"?

177. What famous Irish American said: "You can have any color as long as it's black"?

178. What name is shared by a famous Irish American Olympian and an Irish Socialist leader?

179. Born Elizabeth Cochrane in 1864, she was a journalist and adventurer who went around the world in seventy-two days. By what name is she better known?

180. Identify the speaker of this quote: "Tune in, turn on, drop out."

181. This IRA man served almost nine years in American jails, and his case became a celebrated cause in Irish American circles. In fact, a New York street corner was named after him. Who is he?

182. This Irishman helped establish a company in Cincinnati that began by manufacturing Ivory soap. Name him.

183. The command module pilot of the historic *Apollo 11* moon landing mission never actually set foot on the moon. Who was he?

184. What "Robert" was appointed president of the Ford Motor Company in 1960—the first president of the company who was not a member of the Ford family?

185. Who, while addressing the Irish parliament, included among his qualifications for his claim to be Irish that Barry Fitzgerald was his friend?

186. What U.S.-based Irish organization first proposed the bill to grant twelve thousand U.S. visas to young people in Northern Ireland and the six border counties in the Republic as part of an Irish Peace Process Cultural and Training Program?

187. This former U.S. congressman was sponsor of a visa program designed to give balance and diversity to U.S. immigration policy. The visa program that bears his name was written into the U.S. Immigration Act of 1990. Name the former congressman.

188. What do the Irish American columnists Jimmy Breslin, Anna Quindlen, Jim Dwyer, and Eileen McNamara have in common?

189. Name the priest, born in County Fermanagh, who founded the Irish National Caucus in the United States in 1974.

190. This term, first coined in the United States around 1750, was used to distinguish settlers from the northern counties of Ireland (predominantly Protestant) from other Irish settlers (predominantly Catholic).

191. To whom was the *Chicago Daily News* referring when it reported in 1972, "[She], being female and Irish, is a mystery in her behavior to the British public. They are still mulling deeply over her indecorum in slugging Home Secretary Maulding"?

192. After making history on October 11, 1984, Kathryn D. Sullivan said it was "worth as much as thirty Disneyland E-tickets." What had she just done?

193. James Hoban, an Irish-born architect, won a contest to design this famous U.S. building, construction of which began in 1792. Name the building.

194. Born in Comack, Long Island, this famous Irish American helps charity through sales of a doll that bears her name. Who is she?

FOUR

The Luck o' the Irish in Politics

195. According to the Irish American Heritage Museum, how many American presidents claim Irish heritage?

196. This prominent U.S. politician was named "Irish American of the Year" by *Irish America* magazine in 1996, despite his hazy claims to Irish ancestry.

197. How many U.S. presidents have visited Ireland while in office?

198. What former Boston mayor was arrested and jailed when he was caught taking a civil service postal delivery examination on behalf of an Irish constituent?

199. What was his nickname?

200. Identify the speaker of this quote: "I used to say that politics is the second oldest profession, and I have come to know that it bears a gross similarity to the first."

201. What former Chicago mayor was called "the last of the bosses"?

202. Gerry Adams called him "a lifelong champion of Irish freedom." Who was this Irish-born U. S. civil rights activist who, in 1998, died in New York at the age of ninety-one?

203. What U.S. politician was the recipient of the first annual Paul O'Dwyer Peace and Justice Award in 1998?

204. Name this former speaker of the House of Representatives who had a library in Boston College named after him.

205. Identify the speaker of this quote: "To the people of Northern Ireland I say it is your will for peace, after all, that has brought your country to this moment of hope."

206. What four men were known as the "Four Horsemen" of American politics?

207. Identify the Irish American speaker of this quote: "You can go to hell, and I'm going to Texas."

208. Davy Crockett spent several terms in Congress as a member of what political party?

209. Who was the first Catholic Irish American to hold a cabinet office?

210. What political journalist said: "The mystery of government is not how Washington works but how to make it stop"?

211. In 1928 this Irish American won the Democratic presidential nomination but lost the presidential election to Herbert Hoover when religion became the issue of the campaign. Name him.

212. Name this former Irish American senator from Minnesota who ran for president in 1972, 1976, 1988, and 1992.

213. Name the town in County Tipperary that was home to Ronald Reagan's great-grandfather.

214. An Irish American was responsible for some of the most compassionate and moving speeches of President Reagan, including his response to the 1986 *Challenger* disaster. What was her name?

215. The 1981 attempted assassination of President Reagan took place as he left what hotel?

216. This Irishman was the only Catholic to sign the Declaration of Independence. Who was he?

217. What U.S. president of Irish descent had an Irish setter named King Timahoe?

218. What Irish American wrote *The Boston Irish: A Political History?*

219. Identify the speaker of this quote: "All politics is local."

220. What was the name and political title of the controversial Irish American who attracted national attention that resulted in the eventual coining of the term "McCarthyism"?

221. Name the Irish American who, as mayor of Los Angeles, has a job that few would envy.

222. When he entered Senate office in 1981, he was the youngest elected senator from Connecticut as well as the only Connecticut senator whose father at one time held the same position. Name this Irish American.

223. On December 7, 1993, her son, Kevin, and husband, Dennis, were gunned down on a packed commuter train. In 1996 she was elected to the U.S. Congress. Who is she?

224. In 1998, after a fourteen-year campaign that was strongly opposed by the British government, legislation for fair employment in Northern Ireland was enshrined in U.S. federal law. What is the legislation known as?

225. Identify the speaker of this quote: "As time went on and the countries of the world got closer together,

Ireland seemed to be by itself. Then, all of a sudden, the clouds began to evaporate and Ireland became Ireland."

226. On February 29, 1996, what Irish American was sworn in as the new director of the Office of National Drug Control Policy?

227. What was the name of the antiforeign, anti–Roman Catholic political organization that flourished in the United States between 1852 and 1856?

228. What state elected the highest number of Know-Nothing candidates in the 1854 elections?

229. On September 3, 1998, while speaking in Belfast, whom did President Clinton call "the best investment we ever made in Northern Ireland"?

230. With what U.S. city were notorious political boss Thomas J. Pendergast and his brother, James M. Pendergast, associated?

231. In 1897 James Duval Phelan, without previous political experience, was elected as the first Irish American mayor of what U.S. city?

232. This native of Tyrone, Ireland, was a U.S. general in two different wars (Mexican War and Civil War) and remains the only person in history to represent three different states in the U.S. Senate. Who was he?

233. Who was the first American born of Irish parents to be elected mayor of Boston?

234 This man, who came to Boston from Ireland, was the father of "Honey Fitz." Name him.

The Kennedys

235. What Irish county is the ancestral home of the Kennedy clan?

236. In 1934 what U.S. president appointed Joseph P. Kennedy the first chairman of the Securities and Exchange Commission with the words "It takes a thief to catch a thief"?

237. Who, in 1957, said: "I was born here, my children were born here. What the hell do I have to do to be called an American?"

238. How many of Joseph and Rose Kennedy's sons were elected to the U.S. Senate?

239. What Kennedy based his campaign on the slogan "Kennedy will do more for Massachusetts"?

240. Whose first book, *The Enemy Within*, was published in 1960?

241. John F. Kennedy was the youngest person to be elected president. How old was he?

242. What relation was John F. Kennedy to John "Honey Fitz" Fitzgerald?

243. To what office did President Kennedy appoint his younger bother Bobby?

244. In 1961 what did President Kennedy call on the United States to achieve in the next decade?

245. In what month was John F. Kennedy assassinated?

246. What hospital was President Kennedy rushed to after being shot in Dallas?

247. Who was the Irish American governor of Texas who was seriously wounded during the assassination of President Kennedy?

248. In what cemetery is John F. Kennedy buried?

249. In 1969 Senator Edward Kennedy's car plunged over a bridge at Chappaquiddick and a woman was killed. What was her name?

250. Whose 1987 best-selling biography was entitled *The Fitzgeralds and the Kennedys*?

251. Which Kennedy was accused of rape in 1991 at the family's Palm Beach, Florida, estate after a party?

252. Name the personality-driven, apolitical political magazine that John F. Kennedy Jr. founded in 1995.

253. Her awards include the 1995 Irish American of the Year Award from *Irish America* magazine. Name her.

254. Who delivered the eulogy at the funeral of Rose Kennedy, saying: "Mother knew this day was coming . . . but she did not dread it. She accepted it . . . not as a leaving, but as a returning. She has gone to God. . . ."?

Politics in Ireland

255. Identify the speaker of the quote: "I said in the speech I made earlier I will be a president for all the people. . . . I think it is the role of the president to be president for all people. That's what I intend to be, and that's what I hope to be."

256. Whom did President Clinton call "Ireland's most tireless champion for civil rights and its most eloquent voice of nonviolence"?

257. Hume was one of two recipients of the 1998 Nobel Peace Prize, cited for their work toward ending "the national, religious, and social conflict in Northern Ireland that has cost over 3,500 people their lives." Who was the other recipient?

258. What Irish politician and prominent Ulster Unionist was criticized by other Unionists in 1998 for appearing to suggest that a united Ireland would be a better deal for Unionists than the union with Britain?

259. How many people signed "on behalf of the Provisional Government" the proclamation of the Irish Republic in 1916?

260. After fifty years of misrule and discrimination against the nationalist population, the Northern Ireland parliament was suspended in 1972, whereupon direct rule was imposed from London. Where was the parliament located?

261. What future British prime minister wrote in 1922: "The whole map of Europe has been changed. . . . But as the deluge subsides and the waters fall short we see the dreary steeples of Fermanagh and Tyrone emerging once again. The integrity of their quarrel is one of the few institutions that has been unaltered in the cataclysm which has swept the world"?

262. What is the U.S. government's equivalent of Ireland's Dáil Éireann?

263. Does Ireland have a prime minister, a president, or both?

264. What former Irish president resigned from office in 1997 to take up appointment as United Nations high commissioner for human rights?

265. What do the following Irish political parties have in common: Ulster Unionist Party, Democratic Unionist Party, Ulster Democratic Party, and Progressive Unionist Party?

266. Name the former Irish *taoiseach* (prime minister) who in 1997 was castigated by the Payments to Politicians Tribunal for accepting 1.3 million Irish pounds in gifts from a prominent businessman.

267. An event on November 15, 1985, caused great anger among Ulster Unionists and led to the "Ulster Says No" protests. What was the event?

268. What Irish *taoiseach* (prime minister) signed the Anglo-Irish Agreement of 1985?

269. Article 2 of this document states: "The national territory consists of the whole island of Ireland, its islands and the territorial seas." Name the document.

270. Who was the "rebel countess" who fought with the Irish Citizen Army in 1916 and later branded the Anglo-Irish treaty of 1921 "a betrayal of Republican hopes"?

271. Name the founder and leader of the Irish Transport and General Workers' Union who was on "a divine mission to create discontent."

FIVE
The Irish
Spin on Music

272. This instrument is a "cousin" of the bagpipes that is played while being held under the arm. What is it?

273. What pop singer's real name is Paul Hewson?

274. What group recorded the single "I Don't Like Mondays"?

275. Who wrote Sinead O'Connor's hit single "Nothing compares 2 U"?

276. What kind of animal skin is the handheld drum called the bodhrán traditionally made from?

277. The popular Irish ballad "The Town I Loved So Well" is about what city?

278. Name the Irishman who was one of the main organizers of the Live Aid concerts in 1985.

279. *Hear My Song* is a 1982 movie loosely based on aspects of this Irish tenor's colorful lifestyle.

280. With what Irish group did Bono team up to record the hit "In a Lifetime"?

281. Name the Derry-based group whose members included the O'Neill brothers and Feargal Sharkey.

282. Currently solo, this singer joined Clannad in 1980 and then split with the band in 1982.

283. By what more popular name do we know the singer Declan McManus?

284. For what Irish rock group is Liam O'Maonlai the lead singer?

285. Name the Irish pianist and composer of delicate and expressive piano pieces who invented the nocturne, a new concept in romantic music and precursor to Frédéric Chopin's work in that form.

286. This Irish song is the third most recorded song of all time. Name it.

287. This Irish group, upon invitation by Speaker of the House Thomas "Tip" O'Neill and Senator Edward Kennedy, became the first group to play in the Rotunda of the U.S. Capitol in 1983. Name the group.

288. What is the Gaelic translation for the Irish National Anthem "A Soldier's Song"?

289. Some folks think of "When Johnny Comes Marching Home" as an American song, but it is actually attributed to the Galway-born bandmaster of Benjamin Butler's Union Army, which occupied New Orleans during the Civil War. Who was the bandmaster?

290. Who wrote the popular Irish ballad "A Nation Once Again"?

Well-Known Irish Ballads

Identify these well-known ballads by using the lyrics given.

291. "He counted out his money and it made a pretty penny, I put it in my pocket and I gave it to my Jenny. . . ."

292. "She wore no jewels or costly diamonds, no paint or powder, no none at all. . . ."

293. "But come ye back when summer's in the meadow, or when the valley's hushed and white with snow. 'Tis I'll be there in sunshine or in shadow. . . ."

294. "But the sea is wide and I can't swim over, nor have I the wings to fly. If I could find me a handsome boatman, to ferry me over to my love and die . . ."

295. "By a lonely prison wall, I heard a young girl calling, 'Michael, they are taking you away.' For you stole Trevelyan's corn, so the young might see the morn. Now a prison ship lies waiting in the bay. . . ."

296. "I went to an alehouse I used to frequent, and I told the landlady my money was spent. I asked her for credit, she answered me, 'Nay, such a custom as yours I could have any day.' . . ."

297. "Alone, all alone, by the wave-washed strand, all alone in a crowded hall. The hall it is gay and the waves they are grand, but my heart is not here at all. . . ."

298. "Last night as I lay dreaming of pleasant days gone by, me mind bein' bent on rambling, to Ireland I did fly. . . ."

299. "There's one fair county in Ireland, with memories so glorious and grand. Where nature has lavished its bounty, it's the orchard of Éireann's green land. . . ."

300. "As she pushed her wheelbarrow through streets broad and narrow, crying, 'Cockles and mussels, alive, alive oh!' . . ."

♣ ♣ ♣

301. What world-famous Irish musician—during a rock concert in Belfast where Protestant politician David Trimble and Catholic John Hume took to the stage together and shook hands—led an emotional cry for a "yes" vote in the peace deal referendum in May 1998?

302. Name the band that is widely regarded as the first successful Celtic rock group.

303. What Belfast-based band had among its hits "Alternative Ulster" and "Suspect Device"?

304. Who wrote the popular Irish ballad "Four Green Fields"?

305. Christy Moore wrote a song about what popular Irish music festival?

306. Complete this line from a folk song: "There's a uniform still hanging in what's known as father's room . . ."

307. What is the name of the international organization, with over four hundred branches worldwide, that is dedicated to the advancement of traditional Irish music, language, dance, and culture?

308. Who is widely acclaimed as Ireland's greatest living tenor?

309. Upon its release in Dublin, this album, a collection of classic religious anthems of Ireland, shot straight to number one in the album charts and, in its first three months, went ten times platinum in Ireland alone. Name the album.

310. With what traditional Irish group is Derek Bell usually associated?

311. What is the pop group Culture Club's "Irish connection"?

312. The majority of this group's members are first-generation Irish Americans from the New York area. It is the only all-woman ensemble on the Irish traditional music scene. Name the group.

313. This popular song was included in Bing Crosby's 1944 movie *Going My Way*, where he sang it to a weary Father Fitzgibbon, played by Barry Fitzgerald. Name the song.

314. Name the leader of the Wolfe Tones, who is known for guiding the audience down a magical path as he unfolds the history of Ireland.

315. What Irish city has hosted the world-famous Harp Festival since 1792?

316. Name the well-known Irish musician who shares his name with an Irish county.

317. What entertainer was known for singing these lyrics: "I'm dreaming of a white Christmas . . ."?

318. Among the honors bestowed on this Irish-born tenor during his career was Count of the Holy Roman Empire, in 1928. Name him.

319. From what Broadway musical of the 1960s is the song "How Are Things in Glocca Morra"?

320. Who was the lead singer of the Irish rock band Thin Lizzy, and what instrument did he play?

321. Name the Irish folk band whose repertoire includes "The Unicorn."

322. Name the venue in County Meath that has hosted several large music acts over the years, including Bob Dylan, Queen, Guns n' Roses, and the Verve.

323. Who wrote the song "Give Ireland Back to the Irish," which was banned in Britain?

324. "Early morning, April 4, Shot rings out in the Memphis sky. . . ." What event is being described in this song—"Pride (In the Name of Love)"—by U2?

325. What popular singer has been affectionately nick-named "the Belfast Cowboy"?

326. During his many years as a composer and record producer, he has worked with numerous Irish and international artists, including U2, Van Morrison, Kate Bush, and Paul Brady. His most famous work to date is *River Dance*. Who is he?

327. Name this County Armagh singer, who, along with the Clancy Brothers, helped spark a resurgence of interest in Irish songs and singing in America and Ireland.

328. What is the name of the international music festival that takes place in Rostrevor, County Down, each year?

329. What singer's hits include "Moondance" and "Gloria"?

330. Who, when appearing on Irish American Ed Sullivan's show, could be shown only from the waist up?

331. What Irish singer sparked controversy when she tore up a photograph of the pope?

Who Recorded It?

For each of the following album titles, name the group or artist who recorded it. (Choices: U2, Van Morrison, Hothouse Flowers, Horslips, the Undertones, Four Men & a Dog, Thin Lizzy, Boyzone, Boomtown Rats, the Cranberries)

332. *Enlightenment*

333. *Hypnotised*

334. *Jailbreak*

SIX
Irish on the Silver Screen

342. Who won the Best Supporting Actor Academy Award for his role as a mute in an Irish village in the 1970 film *Ryan's Daughter*?

343. What Irish-born actor received his cinematic "license to kill" in 1994, when he was named the new 007?

344. Who directed the 1930 movie *Juno and the Paycock*, which was based on Sean O'Casey's play?

345. This Irish actress's movies included *Anna Karenina* (1935), *Cardinal Richelieu* (1935), *Pride and Prejudice* (1940), and the Marx Brothers comedy *A Day at the Races* (1937). Name her.

346. Who played Tarzan to Maureen O'Sullivan's Jane?

347. In *Tarzan, the Ape Man* (1932), what was Jane's last name?

348. What was the Irish American star of the *Back to the Future* trilogy?

349. This 1959 movie, set during the Irish rebellion of 1921, starred James Cagney and Richard Harris. Name it.

350. What is perhaps the most obvious Irish connection to the movie *Ben-Hur*?

351. Born in Chicago, the second of five children, this actor was raised by immigrant parents from Birr, Ireland. Name him.

352. In what movie did Quinn play Brad Pitt's character's elder brother?

353. In 1958, to attract offshore productions to Ireland, the government established a film studio facility in Bray, County Wicklow. Name the facility.

354. This 1952 comedy is about an Irish American boxer (played by John Wayne) who comes to Ireland in search of his roots, falls in love with an Irish country lassie, and tames the town bully.

355. In the film, what did the boxer go to Ireland to forget about?

356. And what was his boxing name before he arrived in Ireland?

357. What character did Barry Fitzgerald play in *The Quiet Man*?

358. Name the 1992 movie that starred Samuel L. Jackson as Robby Jackson, Sean Bean as Sean Miller, and Richard Harris as Paddy O'Neil.

359. This Irish American actor starred in the movies *9½ Weeks* and *Barfly*.

360. Rourke, dissatisfied with a 1987 movie in which he starred, directed a personal attack at studio head Sam Goldwyn Jr., saying: "I was making a small movie that I hoped would make things clearer about what's going on [in Northern Ireland]. He wanted to turn it into a big commercial extravaganza-type thing." Name the movie.

361. What was Rourke's character's name in the movie?

362. In what movie did Irish actor Gabriel Byrne star as tough but sentimental Irishman Tom Reagan?

363. Name the Irish author who wrote a trilogy of books—later adapted for the screen—that deal with a Dublin neighborhood and its quirky residents.

364. What film in that trilogy focuses on young Sharon Curley, who is pregnant, unmarried, and determined to have her baby?

365. In *The Commitments,* what legendary soul singer did the title band hope would show up for their make-or-break gig?

366. Name this son of Irish immigrants who won the Oscar for Best Director in 1935, 1940, 1941, and 1952.

367. And which of Ford's movies of 1936 starred Barbara Stanwyck?

368. Who starred as Frank Skeffington, a political boss, in John Ford's 1958 movie *The Last Hurrah?*

369. What sport is featured in the 1963 movie *This Sporting Life?*

370. In the 1990 movie *Darkman,* what Irish actor played the title character?

371. In what Clint Eastwood movie did Neeson play the part of film director Peter Swan?

372. In what 1992 movie does Neeson play a small-town sheriff battling a phony evangelist and his entourage?

373. For what 1982 movie did Peter O'Toole receive a Best Actor Oscar nomination as onetime Hollywood swash-buckler Alan Swann?

374. This 1988 movie was John Huston's last and was scripted by his son, Tony, and based on James Joyce's 1914 short story.

375. Name the Irish-born entertainer who played the title role in the 1972 comedy *Our Miss Fred*.

376. What Irish actor has appeared in *In the Name of the Father, The Secret Garden*, and *Moll Flanders*?

377. In what 1986 movie, set in an Irish border town, did Martin Dempsey appear as a quizmaster?

378. In 1952 he won the Best Actor Golden Globe award for *Singin' in the Rain*. Name this Chicago-born actor, director, and composer who also worked as a conductor, dancer, and circus performer.

379. He married Ava Gardner in 1941, when he was twenty and a big movie star. Name him.

380. Name the Irish actor who starred in the Ireland-based movies *The Boxer* and *In the Name of the Father*.

381. In 1990 Day-Lewis won the Best Actor Academy Award for his role in this film.

382. What actor died shortly after filming for *My Left Foot* ended?

383. How did Irish American (and later princess of Monaco) Grace Kelly die?

384. This Belfast-born actor directed and starred in the 1996 version of William Shakespeare's *Hamlet*. Name him.

385. What Irish actor played Leopold Bloom in the 1967 film version of *Ulysses*?

Irish on the Small Screen

Answer these questions about the Irish on TV.

386. In what TV show did Carroll O'Connor star as Archie Bunker?

387. *Tonight*, starring Johnny Carson, was a nightly way of life for more than a generation. When Carson retired, his loyal sidekick retired, too. Name him.

388. Name the Derry-born actress who stars as Monica, a guardian angel who intervenes in the lives of those in crisis, in *Touched By an Angel*.

389. This television journalist and current affairs show host has provided the running commentary for the New York City St. Patrick's Day parade since 1997. Name her.

390. What was the name of the 1980s TV show in which Irish-born actor Pierce Brosnan played the title character, a sophisticated con man/private investigator?

391. What was the name and title of Colm Meaney's character on *Star Trek: The Next Generation* (which aired from 1987 to 1992)?

392. Before *Star Trek*, Meaney made his feature debut in an obscure sci-fi TV feature in 1986. Name it.

393. What television network broadcast the first bulletin that President Kennedy had been shot in 1963?

394. Jackie Gleason and William Bendix both starred as the dumb father given to moaning, "What a revoltin' development this is," in this 1950s situation comedy. Name the show.

395. In the comedy *Happy Days*, which was set in the mid-1950s, what was the name of the main family?

396. The Irish television comedy *Father Ted* is about three priests who live on a small, somewhat secluded island. Although they are not the best priests in the world, they always mean well. Name the actor who played the part of Father Ted and who passed away in 1998 at the age of forty-five.

397. Name the actor who played Al Bundy in *Married with Children*, a sitcom set in Chicago that parodied the harmonious sitcoms of the mid-1980s.

398. Although he had his own TV show, he is perhaps best remembered for his role as Ralph Kramden in the 1955 series *The Honeymooners*. Name him.

399. Which "Walter" starred as fun-loving Grandpappy Amos in *The Real McCoys*, the 1957 rural comedy about a family of self-reliant hillbillies?

400. In 1954 who called Ed Murrow, host and co-creator of the TV show *See It Now,* "a leader of the jackal pack"?

401. In 1962 who took the American people on a television tour of the White House?

402. His show, originally called *Toast of the Town,* stayed on the air for twenty-three years. Who was this famous show host?

403. Name the forthright and outspoken political chat show host who has acted as a special assistant and speechwriter to Presidents Nixon and Ford.

404. What Irish actor played an IRA man wanted by Scotland Yard in a 1986 episode of *Miami Vice*?

405. Born Joe Yule Jr., he starred as cocky tough kid Mickey McGuire in a series of 1920s short film comedies. In the 1930s he became famous for his role in the *Andy Hardy* series. Who is he?

SEVEN
Name That Film:
The Irish Connection

The questions in this chapter concern movies that were filmed in, based in, or associated with Ireland or Irish America. Given the year and synopsis of each film, can you name each Irish movie? For a bonus point, try to answer each follow-up question.

406. This 1993 film was based on Gerry Conlon's autobiographical novel about "the Guildford Four."

407. In the film, what actress played Conlon's attorney?

408. In this 1992 movie Joseph is a poor tenant farmer who finds himself accompanying his landlord's daughter, Shannon, to America in a quest for land.

409. In what U.S. city did Joseph and Shannon first arrive?

410. The title character of this 1996 film developed techniques of guerrilla warfare that were later copied by leaders of independence movements around the world, from Mao Zedong in China to Yitzhak Shamir in Israel.

411. What character did actor Stephen Rea play in the movie?

412. In this 1997 movie fugitive IRA gunman Rory Devaney is holed up in the home of New York cop Tom O'Meara.

413. What was Devaney's "real name" in the movie?

414. In this 1991 film "Bull" McCabe has a conflict with a wealthy American over a piece of land.

415. How many Academy Award nominations did this movie receive?

416. In this 1992 film Fergus, an IRA man, falls for a woman who is not all that she seems.

417. Who was the only American star in the movie?

418. In this 1990 film a human rights activist's boyfriend is killed by British forces while on a reporting trip of abuses by British Security Forces in Northern Ireland.

419. Name the English detective who was first appointed to investigate the "shoot to kill" policy of British forces in Northern Ireland.

420. In Carole Reed's 1946 thriller, James Mason, playing the part of an injured republican gunman, staggers into a bar to seek sanctuary from a cold and hostile Belfast night.

421. Name the well-known Belfast bar that was featured in the movie.

422. In this 1959 movie an old storyteller's tall tale comes true when he captures the King of the Leprechauns, who grants him three wishes.

423. What is the name of the twenty-one-inch-tall leprechaun in the movie?

424. In this 1991 film concert promoter Micky O'Neill tries to revive a London theater club by booking a Josef Locke impostor.

425. The movie is based on an incident in the life of the world-famous Irish tenor Josef Locke, who fled Britain. What was his reason for fleeing?

426. In this 1988 film financial difficulties lead the owner of an Irish castle to open it as a haunted bed-and-breakfast.

427. What actor's character inherits the ancient Castle Plunkett in the movie?

428. The soundtrack to this 1984 film about the troubles in Northern Ireland was performed by Dire Straits.

429. Who directed the movie?

430. This 1970 film starring Sean Connery was set in 1870s Pennsylvania.

431. What actor played a Pinkerton detective who manages to infiltrate the organization?

432. In this 1998 film Git Hynes is just out of jail, has lost his girlfriend, and finds himself in debt to gangster Tom French, who sends him on an "easy ride" down to Cork to pick up a criminal associate.

433. Name the chatty criminal associate who tries to play off the reluctant chauffeurs against each other.

434. In this 1984 film an undercover British agent is sent to Belfast to apprehend the killer of a British cabinet minister, and a brutal showdown ensues.

435. What Irish group performed the title theme to the movie?

436. Terry George directed this 1996 movie, which is based on the 1981 Irish hunger strikers.

437. Name the two actresses who played the mothers Kathleen Quigley and Annie Higgins in the movie.

438. In this 1986 film unemployed factory workers Vinnie and Arthur build a "wall of death"—a giant barrel in which a motorcyclist can ride horizontally forty feet off the ground.

439. Name the Elvis Presley film that inspired the motorcycle heroes.

440. In this 1929 film Irish tenor John McCormack sings more than a dozen songs, including "Little Boy Blue."

441. Who directed the movie?

442. In this 1986 film Brother Sebastian, struggling with his faith, is moved by the mistreatment of an epileptic ten-year-old in a bleak Irish home for wayward boys on the northeast coast of Ireland.

443. Name the actor who plays Brother Sebastian.

444. In this 1997 romantic comedy by Australian filmmaker Mark Joffe, Marcy Tizard is sent to research her boss's ancestry in Ireland, where she meets a lovable Irish lad.

445. Tizard's boss, John McGlory, is a senator from what U.S. state?

446. In this 1988 comedy we follow Charlie on a nostalgic journey from the time of his youth to a place where he can get even with his stubborn old father.

447. What actor plays Charlie's father?

448. In this 1994 thriller escaped Irish political prisoner and explosives specialist Ryan Gaerity causes mayhem in the city of Boston.

449. What is the name of the boat where the character Gaerity hides out?

450. This 1989 film is based on the autobiography of Christy Brown.

451. My *Left Foot* won two Oscars. Daniel Day-Lewis won for Best Actor. Who won the other?

452. This 1991 film tells the plight of a likable thirty-eight-year-old Chicago policeman who tries to establish his independence from his domineering Irish mother when he falls in love.

453. Name the policeman who was portrayed by actor John Candy.

454. The twenty-seven-year-old writer-director-producer of this 1995 movie won the Grand Jury Prize at Sundance for this debut about "romantic entanglements."

455. How many brothers are in the movie family?

456. Set on the outskirts of Liverpool, this 1986 comedy tells the tale of three different busloads of elderly pensioners—Irish Catholic pensioners, their longtime Protestant adversaries, and a group of senile nursing-home inmates—that descend upon a rundown nightclub to see in the New Year.

457. What popular Irish singer plays the part of the magician Rosco de Ville?

458. In this 1992 film the residents of a small Irish village are enraged by the scandal of a young woman having a baby out of wedlock and refusing to name the father.

459. What actor played the part of local police sergeant Hegarty in the movie?

460. In this 1998 film Sinead O'Connor makes a cameo appearance as the Virgin Mary.

461. Who wrote the award-winning novel upon which the movie is based?

462. This 1995 fairy tale follows the adventures of a small girl who's led to explore the spot where her little brother was swept out to sea years earlier.

463. Name the mythological half-human/half-seal creature who is said to inhabit the nearby island in the movie.

464. This colorful-sounding 1968 movie, in which a leprechaun journeys to the American South to retrieve a stolen pot of gold, was Fred Astaire's last full-length musical role.

465. Who directed *Finian's Rainbow*?

466. In this mystical 1993 movie set in Ireland, Irish actor Gabriel Byrne stars as Papa Reilly, who must raise his two boys in a Dublin slum after the death of his wife.

467. What "first" did the movie mark for Byrne?

468. James Cagney won an Oscar for his role in this 1942 movie, the life of Irish American composer George M. Cohan.

469. What famous director's father played the composer's father in the film?

EIGHT
Telling the Tale: Irish Literature

470. According to the editorial board of Modern Library, a division of Random House, what Irish novel heads the list of the one hundred best English-language novels of the twentieth century?

471. And what novel by F. Scott Fitzgerald is second on the list?

472. What does the "F" in F. Scott Fitzgerald stand for?

473. Upon whose novel was the John Ford movie *The Informer* based?

474. Name the novel by Margaret Mitchell that became a famous movie in 1939.

475. Name the journalist, novelist, author, and screenplay writer who was born in Brooklyn in 1935, of Irish immigrant parents.

476. This Irish poet, essayist, and dramatist was awarded the 1995 Nobel Prize in literature. Name him.

477. Identify the speaker of this quote: "The fickleness of the women I love is only equaled by the infernal constancy of the women who love me."

478. Name the 1998 book by Malachy McCourt that begins with his immigration to the United States from Ireland when he was in his early twenties.

479. This novelist, dramatist, and filmwriter has written the scripts for films based on his novels, including *The Commitments, The Snapper,* and *The Van.* Name him.

480. Identify the speaker of this quote: "Bigamy is having one wife too many. Monogamy is the same."

481. What well-known Irish republican's works include *Falls Memories: A Belfast Life* and *Free Ireland: Towards a Lasting Peace?*

482. Who, upon entering the United States in 1881, told Customs, "I have nothing to declare but my genius"?

483. Born Katherine O'Flaherty in 1850, she wrote more than one hundred short stories in the 1890s. Her 1899 novel, *The Awakening,* was condemned as "poisonous and positively unseemly." Now it is recognized both for the quality of its writing and for its importance as an early feminist work. By what name is O'Flaherty also known?

484. He won the 1983 Pulitzer Prize in poetry for his *Selected Poems*. His other collections of poetry include *Imperfect Thirst*. Who is he?

485. He has become one of the preeminent science-fiction authors since the release of his 1984 novel *Neuromancer*. Considered one of the founders of the "cyberpunk" literary movement, he is credited with coining the term *cyberspace*. Name him.

486. Identify the speaker of this quote: "The test of a first-rate intelligence is the ability to hold two opposed ideas in mind at the same time and still retain the ability to function. . . ."

487. How many Irishmen have won the Nobel Prize in literature?

488. Name them.

489. What Irish American was awarded the 1936 Nobel Prize in literature "for the power, honesty and deep-felt emotions of his dramatic works, which embody an original concept of tragedy"?

490. Whose celebrated 1983 novel *Ironweed* has won great acclaim and was recognized with the Pulitzer Prize?

491. Which of Brendan Behan's plays was set in an Irish brothel?

492. In what century was the *Book of Kells* written?

    a. A.D. 500
    b. A.D. 800
    c. A.D. 1,000

493. What is the subject of the *Book of Kells*?

    a. the history of Ireland
    b. the four gospels
    c. life of St. Patrick

494. Fill in the blank to complete this quote from Jonathan Swift: "Burn everything that comes from England except the _____."

495. In what play by John M. Synge, set near a village on the Mayo coast, does the character Christopher Mahon appear?

496. Who, along with William Butler Yeats, established the Irish Literary Theater in Dublin in 1899?

497. After a devastating fire destroyed the Irish Literary Theater in 1951, a new building was opened on the site in 1966. What is the new building called?

498. Identify the speaker of this quote: "As you can gather from my novel I'm a verbose creature, but I feel nothing short of insanity will ever make me write another line."

499. Name the Irish Romantic poet, born in Dublin in 1779, who wrote *Irish Melodies* (1807–1834), a collection of 130 poems that included such famous titles as "The Last Rose of Summer."

500. This Irish novelist and poet, who was part of the Irish Renaissance, wrote the novel *The Charwoman's Daughter* (1912), which was published in the United States as *Mary, Mary*. Name him.

501. Name the Irish poet and dramatist who, during the late-nineteenth-century Irish cultural revival, urged Irish writers to draw their inspiration directly from Irish life and traditions rather than from English and European sources.

502. He worked on half a dozen hit plays and musicals and wrote radio scripts, screenplays, and dramas. He won the Pulitzer Prize for *Green Pastures* in 1930. Name him.

503. Name the writer who was born in Jacksonville, Illinois, and was jailed during World War II for resisting induction into military service on pacifist grounds.

504. Who was the Georgia-born journalist and author who has secured his place in American literature with his "Uncle Remus" stories?

505. Who wrote the play that was later turned into *My Fair Lady*?

506. Oscar Wilde said that foxhunting was the "unspeakable in pursuit of" what?

507. What novel by Emer Martin tells the story of a sharp-tongued Irish drifter who falls into a darkly comic relationship with Christopher, the "hoodoo man," a Puerto Rican anarchist?

508. Identify the speaker of this quote: "Nothing says more about me than the fact I'm Irish."

509. Of what Irish poet is W. H. Auden speaking in the poem that begins: "He disappeared in the dead of winter, the brooks were frozen, the airports almost deserted . . ."?

510. In *Gulliver's Travels,* what was Gulliver's first name?

511. Who wrote the novels *Rain on the Wind* and *The Silent People*?

512. What playwright said: "I often quote myself. It adds spice to my conversation"?

513. What Irish poet once described the Aran Islands as "the three stepping-stones out of Europe"?

514. Her 1975 suspense novel, *Where Are the Children?*, became a best-seller. Since then she has had many more. Who is she?

515. "Cast a cold eye on life, on death. Horseman, pass by!" On which Irish writer's gravestone does this epitaph appear?

Irish Literary Figures and Their Works

For each of the following literary works, identify the writer. (Choices: Mary McCarthy, Pete Hamill, Thomas Cahill, Eugene O'Neill, John F. Kennedy, Margaret Mitchell, W. B. Yeats, James Joyce, Bram Stoker, George Bernard Shaw, Brendan Behan, Frank McCourt, Flannery O'Connor, Oscar Wilde, Jonathan Swift, John M. Synge, Roddy Doyle, Seamus Heaney, F. Scott Fitzgerald, Maeve Binchy)

516. *Dracula*

517. *Angela's Ashes*

518. *Profiles in Courage*

519. *Long Day's Journey into Night*

520. *A Drinking Life: A Memoir*

521. *Paddy Clarke, Ha Ha Ha*

522. *How the Irish Saved Civilization*

523. *The Spirit Level*

524. *Circle of Friends*

525. *Gone With the Wind*

526. *Arms and the Man*

527. *A Good Man Is Hard to Find*

528. *The Importance of Being Earnest*

529. *Borstal Boy*

530. *A Modest Proposal*

531. *Playboy of the Western World*

532. *The Last Tycoon*

533. *Dubliners*

534. *The Shadowy Waters*

535. *The Group*

The Artist—James Joyce

536. Joyce wrote his poem "Ladies and Gents, You Are Here Assembled from Gas from a Burner" upon the refusal of an Irish firm to publish which of his great works?

537. In September 1888 James Joyce became, at age six, the youngest pupil ever accepted at Ireland's most prestigious school. Name the school.

538. Which of Joyce's works was inspired by the impression left upon him by a religious retreat and a priest's sermons?

539. Upon graduation from University College, Dublin, Joyce left Ireland to attend medical school. What city did he go to?

540. The publication of this Joyce novel was halted by a U.S. court in 1920 because it was considered "obscene." Name the novel.

541. Under what name would Joyce's "Work in Progress" later be published?

542. Fill in the blank to complete this quote of Joyce: "Six years ago (at sixteen) I left the _____, hating it most fervently. I found it impossible for me to remain in it on account of the impulses of my nature."

543. What Irish nationalist leader was a blood relation of Joyce?

544. From what was James Joyce suffering when he died on January 13, 1941?

NINE
The Irish Take on Sports

545. He helped organize major league baseball's American League, became the owner and president of the Chicago White Sox, and, in 1939, was elected to the National Baseball Hall of Fame. Who was he?

546. Who was known as the "Boston Strong Boy"?

547. Whom did John L. Sullivan lose to in the first heavyweight championship under the marquis of Queensberry rules?

548. Of what famous 1942 movie was Corbett the subject?

549. In which New York City borough is Gaelic Park, a facility for Gaelic sports such as Gaelic football?

550. Name the winner and runner-up at the 1982 Wimbledon Men's Singles Championship.

551. What Irish boxer was nicknamed the "Clones Cyclone"?

552. Name the Irishman who won the world snooker championship in 1985.

553. Name the Irish jockey who rode "Grundy" to victory in both the Irish and English Derbys in 1975.

554. In 1953 she became the first woman to win the tennis grand slam, taking first place in the U.S. Open, Australian Open, French Open, and Wimbledon.

555. In 1987, at the age of twenty-seven, he became the first Irishman to win the Tour de France bicycle race. To date he is the only Irishman to accomplish the feat. Who is he?

556. During the heyday of the bathhouses, this place was a popular destination for professional boxers, who found the mineral waters a beneficial part of their training programs.

557. In June 1986 featherweight Barry McGuigan lost his WBA title in the 129-degree heat of Las Vegas. Who was his opponent?

558. Name the Irish swimmer who won three gold medals in swimming at the Atlanta Olympic Games.

559. In what three events did she win gold?

560. Not including a prologue time trial, how many stages of the Tour de France did Ireland host in 1998?

561. Irish Draught and Irish Hunter are breeds of what type of animal?

562. In November 1996 Notre Dame recorded its thirty-third straight victory over Navy, establishing a new NCAA record for consecutive victories by one school over another. What was the venue for the history-making game?

563. In August 1998 Formula One racing team Jordan Grand Prix scored the first victory of its 126-race career, which began in 1991. At what Grand Prix did it make history?

Sports Stars—Past and Present

Name the sport most associated with each of the following Irish sports stars (choices: Gaelic football, soccer, American football, golf, boxing, rowing, show jumping, Formula One racing, snooker, athletics, rugby, baseball, steeplechase).

564. Pat Jennings

565. Tony Ward

566. Wayne McCullough

567. Eddie Irvine

568. Sonia O'Sullivan

569. Steve Collins

570. George Farran

571. Eddie Macken

572. Roger Bresnahan

573. John Caldwell

574. Darren Clarke

575. Willie John McBride

576. Jonjo O'Neill

577. David O'Leary

578. John "Old Smoke" Morrissey

579. Pat Spillane

580. Niall O'Toole

581. Tony Rice

582. Eamonn Coughlan

583. What is Ireland's best known racecourse?

    a. the Curragh
    b. Galway
    c. Epsom

584. In greyhound races, what do the dogs run after?

    a. a badger
    b. a rabbit
    c. a fake hare

585. What horse race usually takes place in Ireland in June?

    a. the Derby
    b. the Grand National
    c. King George and Queen Elizabeth Stakes

586. Approximately how many golf courses are there in Ireland?

      a. 200
      b. 300
      c. 500

587. In what year did Ireland first qualify for the finals of the soccer World Cup?

      a. 1969
      b. 1979
      c. 1989

588. In what sport does an Irish team play in the Five Nations Cup?

      a. soccer
      b. rugby
      c. handball

589. What Irish boxer won a gold medal in the Barcelona Olympics?

      a. Stephen Collins
      b. Barry McGuigan
      c. Michael Carruth

590. In what event did Irish athlete John Tracy win an Olympic silver medal in Los Angeles in 1984?

      a. 1,500 meters
      b. 5,000 meters
      c. marathon

591. What event did Irish cyclist Sean Kelly win in 1988?

    a. Tour de France
    b. Tour of Spain
    c. Circuit of Ireland

592. At the Atlanta Olympics, the Irish foursome of Neville Maxwell, Tony O'Connor, Sam Lynch, and Derek Holland came in fourth in what event?

593. Whom did Ayrton Senna punch after a pit lane argument at the 1993 Japanese Grand Prix?

594. In what sport would you use a *sliotar* and a *caman*?

595. Name the Irish American athlete from Boston who was the first Olympic gold medalist of modern times.

596. What type of animal was the famous Irish "Master M'Grath"?

597. During his career, he was Irish champion jockey seven times and won all the big races in Ireland. He also won the Epsom Derby, Epsom Oaks, and the French Derby. Name this Irish jockey who retired in 1998 at the age of forty-eight.

598. In what outdoor activity did Eddie Cooper of Belfast make history in 1998?

599. He joined the Boston Celtics during the 1979–80 season and guided a team that won twenty-nine games the year before to sixty-one victories in his rookie campaign. Name this Boston Celtics legend.

600. Who were the "Big Three" of the Boston Celtics in the 1980s?

601. Name the 1996 movie—starring Damon Wayans, Daniel Stern, and Dan Aykroyd—in which a fanatical fan tries to help the Boston Celtics win the NBA championship by kidnapping the Utah Jazz's superstar player.

602. The "Manassa Mauler" became world heavyweight champion in 1919 and fought a total of sixty-nine professional fights in his career, with forty-seven wins by knockout. Who was he?

603. What epithet was applied to Dempsey's right hand?

604. Whom did Dempsey lose the heavyweight boxing title to in 1926?

605. In his second fight with Gene Tunney, why did the referee delay the count when Dempsey knocked Tunney down in the seventh round?

606. In 1928 he was awarded the American League MVP, and for eleven consecutive years during the late 1920s and early 1930s, he caught over one hundred games per season. In 1947 he was elected to the National Baseball Hall of Fame. Name him.

607. With what category of sport is the "Sullivan Award" associated?

608. What Irish sporting organization has its headquarters at Croke Park, Dublin?

609. What horse race was the first in history to be broadcast live by satellite to the United States from Ireland?

610. Often referred to as "Baseball's first superstar," he was born December 31, 1857, in Troy, New York. He made his major league debut on May 1, 1878, and died in Boston on November 8, 1894. Who was he?

611. What happened to Roger Bresnahan, Jimmy Collins, Hugh Duffy, King Kelly, and Jim O'Rourke in 1945?

612. Name the popular turn-of-the-century fighter who is credited with inventing the "corkscrew punch," which is thrown while rotating the fist.

613. Paul Morphy played 227 competitive games during his lifetime, winning 83 percent of them. What were these games that he became famous for playing?

614. How did Nolan Ryan make Texas Rangers' history in September 1996?

615. What sport did Michael Phelan help to popularize in the late 1800s, a sport at which he became the U.S. "champion" in 1859, according to promoters?

616. He won four national football championships and coached four Heisman Trophy winners at Notre Dame. He resigned in 1954 for health reasons and died of leukemia in 1973. He is commemorated with a bronze sculpture outside Notre Dame Stadium. Who is he?

617. Name the Irish soccer player—one of the world's best—who played for Los Angeles, Ft. Lauderdale, and San Jose in the North American Soccer League in the late seventies and early eighties.

618. For what Irish sport is the Liam McCarthy Cup awarded?

619. In what year was Jack Charlton appointed manager of the Irish national soccer team?

> **a.** 1982
> **b.** 1984
> **c.** 1986

620. Who scored the memorable goal in the Rebublic of Ireland's defeat of Italy in the 1994 World Cup Soccer Finals?

621. In what sport did partners McNamara and McNamee compete?

622. Who was the owner of the Dodgers baseball franchise who moved the team from Brooklyn to Los Angeles in 1958?

623. What Irish boxer is nicknamed the "Pocket Rocket" for his furious fighting style?

624. What boxer was awarded the Edward J. Neil Trophy for "Fighter of the Year" in 1938 and the James J. Walker Award for "Long and Meritorious Service to Boxing" in 1957?

625. What do Troy, Shahrastani, St. Jovite, Assert, and Shergar have in common?

626. The Irish Derby takes place every year at the Curragh, which is in what county?

627. What record-breaking baseball slugger said: "Maybe . . . I'll go back [to Ireland] someday when I'm retired"?

628. What famous racehorse was kidnapped in 1983, never to be seen again?

TEN

The Fighting Irish:
Irish in the Military

629. Name this son of Ulster emigrants who led the decisive defeat of the British at the Battle of New Orleans.

630. What was the name of the Irish quick-step that was adopted by Custer's Seventh Cavalry Regiment as their official air (tune)?

631. After the Cuban missile crisis, President Kennedy remarked: ". . . the military are mad. They wanted to do this [invade]. It's lucky for us that we have _____ over there [in the Department of Defense]." Fill in the blank.

632. This Civil War brigade was composed of Union army regiments from New York, Massachusetts, and Pennsylvania. What was the brigade commonly known as?

633. In what state did Colonel James A. Mulligan lead an Irish American outfit?

634. Father William Corby, chaplain of the Irish Brigade, became the first president of what famous American institution after the war?

635. During the Mexican War, what was the name of the hard-fighting Mexican army unit that was composed of Irish deserters from the U.S. Army?

636. What Irish American (whose statue stands at CIA headquarters) was director of the Office of Strategic Services, the forerunner of the CIA?

637. What is unique about William Donovan in U.S. military circles?

638. What Confederate general, born in County Cork, was nicknamed "Stonewall Jackson of the West"?

639. What was the number of John F. Kennedy's torpedo boat during World War II?

640. What Irish-born naval commander boasts the epithet "Father of the American Navy"?

641. What famous liberty ship, built in 1943, was named in honor of the Machias seaman who led the rebel raid on the HMS *Margaretta* on the Machias River (in Maine) in the first naval battle of the American Revolution?

642. How did the *O'Brien* make history in 1994?

643. What World War II fighter pilot gave his life for his country and his name to the busiest airport in the world in 1949?

644. Who was the chaplain of the "Fighting 69th" (Sixty-ninth New York Volunteers) during World War I?

645. This member of the Tennessee militia spent several terms in Congress and died when the Alamo fell. Name this Irish American.

646. This man took an active part in the American Revolution, served as a U.S. senator in the first Congress, and was reputedly the richest man in America when he died. Name him.

647. Approximately how many Medals of Honor were awarded to Irish-born U.S. soldiers between 1861 and 1914?

> **a.** 200
> **b.** 500
> **c.** 750

648. Approximately how many Irish-born soldiers fought in the Union army during the American Civil War?

> **a.** 100,000
> **b.** 120,000
> **c.** 160,000

649. Name the man who, during World War I, toured German POW camps and recruited some fifty Irish prisoners (captured as members of British units) to form the nucleus of an Irish brigade to fight on the German side.

650. For what is Captain John Reilly (from the Clifden area of Galway) best remembered during the Mexican war?

651. As part of the Treaty of Limerick in 1691, the Irish forces who fought against the army of William of Orange sailed to France to join King James II in exile. Who was the leader of the Irish forces?

652. What Union army officer defied an order to parade his Sixty-ninth Militia for the Prince of Wales in 1860?

653. During this battle—the first major battle of the Civil War—Lieutenant Colonel James Haggerty was killed in action and Colonel Corcoran was taken a prisoner of the Confederates. Name the battle.

654. During the Civil War, the flags of most Irish regiments were green and predominantly emblazoned with what symbol?

655. Name the high king of Ireland whose forces, along with allies, defeated the Vikings at the Battle of Clontarf in 1014 and returned the land of Ireland to the Irish.

656. Which of John F. Kennedy's brothers died when his aircraft exploded over the English Channel in 1944?

657. As a nurse, she accompanied the First Michigan Cavalry during the Civil War and remained with the U.S. Army as a laundress after the war. Soldiers nicknamed her "Irish Bridget" or "Michigan Bridget." Who was she?

658. What is the family name of the five brothers from Iowa who died together during World War II when a torpedo fired from a Japanese submarine struck the USS *Juneau*?

659. Name the Irishman who enlisted in the U.S. Navy on March 17, 1862, and was awarded the Medal of Honor for his courageous stand in helping to turn back the fierce Confederate assault at Yazoo City, Mississippi, in 1864.

660. A leader of the 1848 "Young Ireland" rebellion, this man was condemned to death, reprieved, exiled to Tasmania, and escaped to the United States, where he practiced law, published a newspaper, and gained a reputation as an orator. Who was he?

661. What is the connection between Irish American Matthew Brady and the American Civil War?

662. What country did the American Fenians attack in an attempt to gain leverage in persuading the British to leave Ireland?

663. Who was the Irish American Nazi propagandist who broadcast via radio to England during World War II?

664. He was born in 1777 in Foxford, County Mayo. When he was nine years old his family left for Boston, and he began a career at sea that would eventually lead to his setting up the Argentinian navy. Name him.

665. This Irish descendant was Chile's liberator and, upon defeating the Spanish in 1817, was elected supreme director of Chile.

666. The Union forces called it the Battle of Antietam. In the South it was called the Battle of Sharpsburg. However, on September 17, 1862, it is estimated that over five hundred of the Irish Brigade lay dead or wounded after this famed battle. In what U.S. state did it occur?

667. His thirty-eight enemy kills made him the second leading American fighter pilot of World War II. An air force base in his home state of New Jersey was named in his honor. Who was he?

668. In what U.S. city do municipal and state workers get St. Patrick's Day off, to officially commemorate the evacuation of the British from the city?

669. Since its introduction during the Civil War, this award has been bestowed upon over two hundred Irish immigrants, more than any other immigrant group in the United States. Name the award.

670. This Irish American was the most decorated U.S. soldier of World War II, winning more than twenty medals (including the Medal of Honor) while fighting in North Africa, Italy, France, Germany, and Austria—all before the age of nineteen. Name him.

671. In 1955 Murphy starred as himself in the film adaptation of his own best-selling autobiography. Name the film.

672. A famous quote reads: "England's difficulty is Ireland's opportunity." Name the Irish American organization that conspired to have Germany aid the Irish nationalists in the 1916 Easter Rising.

673. The flag of the Irish Brigade's Sixty-third New York Regiment was adorned with a gold harp. What was directly below the harp on the flag?

ELEVEN
Irish Stew: General Irish Knowledge

674. What is the Gaelic name for Ireland?

675. What did the Romans call Ireland?

676. The southern part of Ireland has had three official state names since partition. What are they?

677. What is lignite?

678. Fill in the blank: The Irish have been called a nation of "_____ keepers."

679. The oldest political party in Ireland takes its name from the Irish Gaelic expression "We Ourselves." Name the party.

680. What is the "Celtic Tiger"?

681. What is the punt?

682. Approximately what percentage of people living in Ireland have relations in the United States?

      a. 10 percent
      b. 20 percent
      c. 30 percent

683. Approximately how many people of Irish descent are there worldwide?

      a. 50 million
      b. 70 million
      c. 90 million

684. Twenty-eight people died and more than two hundred were injured when a car bomb exploded on Saturday, August 15, 1998. In which town did this, Northern Ireland's biggest single loss of life in the "Troubles," occur?

685. How did sixty-seven-year-old hermit Sister Frances Meigh make history in County Louth, Ireland, in 1998?

686. Irish MEP (Member of European Parliament) Mary Banotti is the grandniece of what famous Irish historical figure?

687. In 1998 Bertie Ahern became the first Irish *taoiseach* (prime minister) to visit this country since Ireland established diplomatic relations with it in 1979. Name the country.

688. This Belfast hotel has the distinction of being the most bombed hotel in Europe. Name it.

689. What Irish natural phenomenon is a volcanic rock formation consisting of thousands of closely placed, polygonal pillars of black basalt?

690. What lies between Mizen Head and Malin Head?

691. What did Ernest Walton, a scientist from Waterford, win in 1951?

692. The IRA declared its first cease-fire in 1994. During the following year, approximately how many people from the Republic of Ireland visited Northern Ireland?

> **a.** 170,000
> **b.** 270,000
> **c.** 470,000

Irish—It's in the Name

Using the following clues, identify the two-word phrases that begin with the word *Irish*.

693. This hot drink includes Irish whiskey and is topped with whipped cream.

694. This high-count cloth is handmade in Ireland and is used for making tablecloths and handkerchiefs.

695. This dish is usually made from meat with potatoes, onions, and other vegetables.

696. This tree, *Taxus baccata stricta,* of Eurasia and northern Africa, has upright branches and dark green foliage with color variations.

697. This Irish breed of dog stands approximately eighteen inches high at the shoulder and has a dense, wiry reddish coat.

698. This is an extinct deerlike mammal; the male of the species had antlers that grew up to thirteen feet in length.

699. This is a paradoxical statement that appears at first to make sense.

700. This purplish brown seaweed grows off the Atlantic coasts of Europe and North America.

701. This marine fish can be found from Alaska to Northern California.

702. This sturdy woolen fabric is made in Ireland and is used for making suits and blankets.

♣ ♣ ♣

703. What fossil fuel does the Irish agency Bord na Móna mainly oversee?

704. This Irish ring displays a heart with a crown above it and a pair of hands encircling it. What is the name of this ring?

705. Which aspect of the Claddagh ring symbolizes loyalty?

706. In what Irish county is the small fishing village of Claddagh, supposedly where the Claddagh ring originated?

707. What famous Irish castle was built by Cormac McCarthy?

708. The Rose of Tralee International Festival draws families from across the world to Ireland for entertainment, pageantry, and fun. At this festival, a young woman of Irish birth or ancestry is chosen to become the "Rose of Tralee." In what Irish county is the festival held?

709. What Irish garment is made of stitches with names like "Tree of Life," "The Bobailín" ("The Blackberry"), and "Crab's Claw"?

710. Ireland's oldest traditional fair is the Oul' Lammas Fair. In what town is it annually held?

711. The "unsinkable" *Titanic* (of recent movie fame) was actually built in Belfast. How many "sister" ships did the *Titanic* have?

712. The Irish police force is commonly known as "Garda." What is its full name?

713. Derry school, St. Columb's College, assumed a world record in 1998 by becoming the only school in the world capable of boasting what?

714. In October of 1997 the oldest footprints in the Northern Hemisphere were discovered on an island off the coast of County Kerry. Name the island.

715. What American country-western superstar, when asked about his Irish concerts in 1998, said, "I said I would come and here I am, a man of my word. It isn't any kind of peace mission. I'm just glad to be making it to Belfast. The Irish, from both sides of the border, have been sweet to me."

716. The flax plant, often described as "the wee blue blossom," is the source of what Irish product associated worldwide with quality and skill?

717. What two months are typically Ireland's sunniest?

718. Name the ocean current system that is largely responsible for the lack of extreme summer heat and winter cold in Ireland.

719. Who is the archbishop of Armagh and Irish cardinal who published the first autobiography by an Irish bishop since St. Patrick wrote his *Confessio*?

720. What is the largest Protestant denomination in Ireland?

721. What is the approximate Roman Catholic population of Ireland?

> **a.** 3 million
> **b.** 4 million
> **c.** 5 million

722. How many varieties of snake are there in Ireland?

723. The Irish Republic occupies what percentage of the island of Ireland?

> **a.** 65 percent
> **b.** 75 percent
> **c.** 85 percent

724. Covering an area of one acre, this Irish landmark is one of the most impressive prehistoric monuments in Europe.

725. What Irish city's Gaelic name translates to "Town of the Ford of the Hurdles"?

726. What is the name of the agency that, since 1994, has been responsible for licensing the categories of development that have the greatest potential to cause pollution in Ireland?

727. What type of rock is the Blarney stone?

728. When Charles Lindbergh made the first solo transatlantic flight to Paris in 1927, what part of Ireland did he see first?

729. There was a lot riding on John Boyd Dunlop's invention in Belfast in 1889. What was the invention?

730. In Ireland, groups of "strawboys" went around acting out traditional plays and songs at Christmas and other times of the year, expecting to be rewarded with food and drink for the entertainment they offered. By what other name are they known?

Irish Food and Drink

731. What process was brought to Ireland, probably from the Middle East, by missionary monks in about A.D. 600?

732. By the latter part of the eighteenth century, approximately how many pot stills were making whiskey in Ireland?

> **a.** 500
> **b.** 1,000
> **c.** 2,000

733. In the United States, corned beef and cabbage is a very popular dish, especially on St. Patrick's Day. However, it is typically not a popular dish in Ireland. What is its nearest equivalent in Ireland?

734. Before Prohibition, approximately how many brands of Irish whiskey were on sale in the United States?

      a. 200
      b. 400
      c. 600

735. The traditional dish "Dublin coddle" contains what type of meat?

736. Midelton, County Cork, is reputedly home to the world's largest what?

737. What was a griddle traditionally used for?

738. What Irish whiskey company boasts that the contents of each bottle comes "from the world's oldest whiskey distillery"?

739. Which two brands of stout are brewed in Cork, Ireland?

740. Irish stew is a very popular dish in Ireland and around the world. In fact, there are probably as many varieties of it as there are Irish counties! Which meat is traditionally used in its preparation?

741. An old poem says, "Boxty on the griddle, boxty in the pan,/If you can't make boxty, you'll never get a man." What is the main ingredient of "boxty"?

742. What vegetable traditionally gives "champ" its distinctive flavor?

743. This famous Irish beverage was named after a bar in Dublin that was a favorite haunt of James Joyce's. Some say that it originated from a tradition in the west of Ireland, where one "dropped a dab of fresh cream into some Irish whiskey, stirred, shook, and tossed it down." Name the drink.

744. What is the world's best-selling Irish whiskey today?

745. "Colcannon" is a popular dish of which there are several versions. If one version consists of mashed potatoes mixed with onions and butter, what main vegetable ingredient is missing?

746. Each year, on the last weekend of September, thousands of people gather to celebrate the height of the Atlantic oyster season in this world-famous festival. In what Irish city is it held?

747. In 1996, based on per-capita consumption, Ireland was the world's largest consumer of what breakfast cereal?

748. What ingredient is used to sweeten Irish Mist liqueur?

749. What type of fish is used to make the dish "Dublin lawyer"?

750. An old Irish verse goes: "Did you treat your Mary Ann,/To dulse and yellow man,/At the Ould Lammas Fair in Ballycastle-O?" What is "dulse," and what is "yellow man"?

Answers

CHAPTER ONE. Ireland Through the Ages: Irish History

1. Protestant Ascendancy

2. tithe

3. Penal Laws

4. Society of United Irishmen

5. Vinegar Hill (outside Enniscorthy)

6. b. seventeenth

7. Saint Brendan (An epic modern voyage led by Tim Severin in the 1970s showed that it was possible to sail a small boat made of wood and leather to America and, consequently, that Irish monks might indeed have preceded Christopher Columbus by several centuries.)

8. 1847 ("Black 47")

9. Charles Trevelyan

10. *Times of London* (The *Times* reckoned that the famine would rid England of Irish discontent.)

11 c. 8 million (It has been estimated that at the start of the nineteenth century, Ireland's population was about 5.4 million. This grew to about 8.2 million by the early 1840s, just before the famine. By the end of the century the figure was down to about 4.5 million.)

12. Gerry Adams

13. Bobby Sands (Sands was a political activist who died in a Northern Ireland prison in May 1981, which ended his sixty-five-day hunger strike.)

14. Easter Proclamation/Irish Declaration of Independence (Approximately one thousand copies of the proclamation are thought to have been printed at Liberty Hall in Dublin. The original document was destroyed in the 1916 Easter Rising.)

15. Orange Order (University of Ulster researchers believe that membership is likely to have hit a maximum of one hundred thousand in the early part of this century but has shrunk to less than half that.)

16. Clifden

17. Betty Williams and Mairead Corrigan

18. Sean McBride

19. He was captured by pirates and sold as a slave.

20. a. fifth (St. Patrick was ordained a bishop in A.D. 432. So where does the story about Saint Patrick driving the snakes out of Ireland come from? Snakes being commonly associated with Satan, sin, and evil since the Garden of Eden, this tale may have arisen as a metaphor of his single-handed effort to drive the idol-worshiping Druid cult out of Ireland.)

21. Earl Louis Mountbatten

22. Tara

23. Margaret Thatcher (Thatcher was talked out of the idea by cabinet ministers.)

24. John Hume

25. Sean MacBride

26. King George V

27. James Connolly (Connolly was so seriously wounded during the Rising that he had to be strapped into a chair in order to be executed.)

28. Horatio Nelson

29. Pope John Paul II

30. Sir Edward Carson

31. Airey Neave

32. Black and Tans

33. the Normans

34. Fourteen

35. Howth

36. He got married.

37. King William III (William of Orange)

38. Ireland never joined NATO

39. Harry Boland

40. linen industry

41. John Hume

42. Whiddy Island

Irish Folklore and Mythology

43. shoemaker

44. "the gift of the gab" (eloquence)

45. Finn McCool

46. Bran

47. Oscar

48. Cuchulainn

49. one (Connla)

50. Lir

51. Banshee, or *Bean-sidhe* (Irish for "Fairy woman")

52. Queen Maeve

53. Mermaid (Her presence always ensures a storm or a disaster at sea. When a sailor fails to come home from the sea, it is sometimes said that he "married a mermaid.")

54. silkies

55. the Burren

56. fairies, or *sidhe* (pronounced "shee")

57. the Fianna

CHAPTER TWO. From Mizen Head to Malin Head: Irish Geography

58. Thirty-two

59. Antrim

60. Wicklow

61. Wales

62. River Shannon (230 miles long)

63. Carrantuohill, County Kerry (3,415 feet)

64. Scotland (Mull of Kintyre)

65. Belfast

66. Meath

67. River Foyle

68. the Mourne Mountains ("the Mountains of Mourne")

69. Slieve Donard (2,796 feet)

70. Leitrim (approximately 2.5 miles)

71. Belfast

72. Antrim

Irish Waterways

73. River Lee

74. River Liffey

75. River Foyle

76. River Lagan

77. River Boyne

78. Ulster Canal

79. River Nore

80. River Blackwater

81. River Bann

82. River Suir

83. River Suir (114 miles long)

84. Mayo

85. Clare

86. Mount Errigal

87. Clare

88. Mayo

89. Aran Islands

90. three

91. Inishmór, Inishmaan, and Inisheer

92. Louth

93. Donegal

94. Carrantuohill

95. Carlow

96. three (Mayo, Meath, and Monaghan)

97. Kerry

98. four

99. Ulster, Leinster, Munster, and Connaught

100. Ulster

101. Lough Neagh (147 square miles)

102. c. 300 miles

103. four

104. Atlantic Ocean, North Channel, Irish Sea, St. George's Channel

105. Antrim Mountains

106. Derry

107. Down

108. Armagh

109. east

110. Cork

111. Lough Derg (in County Donegal)

112. the Burren

113. Clare

114. Achill Island (off the coast of County Mayo)

115. nine (Antrim, Armagh, Cavan, Derry, Donegal, Down, Fermanagh, Monaghan, and Tyrone)

Irish Counties

116. County Louth

117. County Kerry

118. County Armagh

119. County Cork

120. County Meath

121. County Fermanagh

122. County Sligo

123. County Tipperary

124. County Clare

125. County Roscommon

126. Iceland

127. Armagh

128. basalt

129. the Ice Age

130. Antrim

131. Newry Canal (in County Down)

132. O'Connell Street (It was named O'Connell Street after "the Liberator," Daniel O'Connell.)

133. Antrim

134. Kildare

135. c. 105 miles

136. Donegal

137. b. Lough Corrib

138. five (Antrim, Armagh, Derry, Down, and Tyrone)

139. true

CHAPTER THREE. The Irish Across the Atlantic: Irish America

140. Massachusetts (Approximately 40 percent of the population is believed to be of Irish descent.)

141. Buffalo Bill

142. Joseph P. Kennedy Sr.

143. Savannah, Georgia (In 1961, the organizers of the Savannah parade were the first to dye their river green. However, the water was so choppy that the river—or only part of it—became merely greenish, rather than brilliant green. The mayor of Chicago at the time called to ask if his city could dye its river green. He was, of course, given permission to do so, and the annual greening of the Chicago River continues to this day.)

144. 1850s (over 900,000 people)

145. b. 33 percent (This was the largest foreign-born group, followed closely by the Germans.)

146. New Hampshire

147. Maine (33,265 square miles)

148. c. twelve

149. Pennsylvania

150. Brooklyn Bridge

151. St. Patrick's Cathedral, New York

152. John F. Kennedy

153. c. 40 million

154. Presbyterian

155. b. 1892

156. Annie Moore

157. Elizabeth Gurley Flynn ("Rebel Girl" Elizabeth Gurley Flynn was a Socialist and labor movement activist who dedicated her life to defending the rights of U.S. workers until her death in September 1964.)

158. Butte, Montana

159. *Irish Echo*

160. Orange Order

161. b. 7 million

162. Ancient Order of Hibernians (Founded in New York in 1836, the order can trace its roots back to the Irish Ancient Order of Hibernians, which has existed in Ireland for over three hundred years.)

163. Irish Republican Brotherhood, or Fenians (In 1858 Stephens helped form the Fenian Brotherhood in America. He later returned to Ireland to found the Irish Republican Brotherhood.)

164. first American cardinal (He was also, of course, the first Irish American to hold the position.)

165. Nebraska

166. Joseph Kennedy

167. Maine

168. Elizabeth Gurley Flynn

169. the Irish American Partnership

170. John Ireland

171. Tony O'Reilly

172. Jackie Kennedy

173. George "Bugs" Moran

174. Bill Flynn

175. Charles Dion "Deanie" O'Banion

176. New Orleans

177. Henry Ford

178. James Connolly

179. Nellie Bly

180. Timothy Leary (Leary, once a professor of psychology at Harvard, became famous for his advocacy of LSD experimentation and other forms of social activism.)

181. Joe Doherty

182. James Gamble (of Procter & Gamble)

183. Michael Collins

184. Robert McNamara

185. Ronald Reagan

186. Irish Immigration Reform Movement

187. Bruce Morrison (Morrison represented the Third District of Connecticut in the House of Representatives from 1983 until 1991. In 1994 he led a delegation of Irish Americans to Ireland, which played a key role in engineering a cease-fire by the Irish Republican Army in the long-running conflict in Northern Ireland.)

188. All have won the Pulitzer Prize (for commentary)

189. Father Sean McManus

190. "Scotch-Irish"

191. Bernadette Devlin

192. She became the first American woman to walk in space.

193. the White House

194. Rosie O'Donnell

CHAPTER FOUR. The Luck o' the Irish in Politics

195. nineteen

196. Bill Clinton

197. four (Kennedy in 1963, Nixon in 1970, Reagan in 1984, and Clinton in 1995 and 1998)

198. James Michael Curley (In addition to serving four terms as mayor of Boston, Curley served two terms in Congress and one as governor of Massachusetts. His headstone reads, "The Mayor of the poor.")

199. "the Purple Shamrock"

200. Ronald Reagan

201. Richard Daley (Daley was mayor from 1955 to 1976 and belonged to one of Illinois's most famous political family dynasties.)

202. Paul O'Dwyer (O'Dwyer, who was born in County Mayo, was a former New York City council president and New York City commissioner to the United Nations.)

203. Bill Clinton

204. Thomas Phillip "Tip" O'Neill Jr. (In 1952 he ran for the United States House of Representatives and was elected to the seat once held by John F. Kennedy. Tip O'Neill never forgot his ethnic roots. He once explained that he grew up in an atmosphere where he knew he was Irish before he knew he was American.)

205. Bill Clinton

206. Ted Kennedy, Tip O'Neill, Hugh Carey, and Daniel Patrick Moynihan

207. Davy Crockett

208. Democratic Party

209. Joseph McKenna (attorney general, 1897)

210. P. J. O'Rourke

211. Alfred E. Smith

212. Eugene McCarthy

213. Ballyporeen

214. Peggy Noonan

215. the Washington Hilton

216. Charles Carroll III

217. Richard Nixon

218. Thomas O'Connor

219. Tip O'Neill

220. Joseph McCarthy, U.S. senator

221. Richard Riordan

222. Senator Christopher Dodd

223. Carolyn McCarthy

224. MacBride Fair Employment Principles

225. Paul O'Dwyer

226. General Barry R. McCaffrey

227. the Know-Nothing Party (It was known as such because members answered, "I know nothing," when asked about their exclusive, native-Protestant organization.)

228. Massachusetts

229. Senator George Mitchell

230. Kansas City

231. San Francisco

232. James Shields (1806–1879)

233. John "Honey Fitz" Fitzgerald ("Honey Fitz" was also the first Irish American congressman from Boston.)

234. Thomas Fitzgerald

The Kennedys

235. Wexford

236. Franklin D. Roosevelt

237. Joseph P. Kennedy (*New York Times*, January 28, 1957)

238. three (John, Edward, and Robert)

239. John (in his Senate race against the Republican incumbent, Henry Cabot Lodge Jr.)

240. Robert Kennedy (The book dealt with his investigations of Jimmy Hoffa and other organized crime figures.)

241. Forty-three

242. grandson

243. attorney general

244. land a man on the moon

245. November (November 22, 1963)

246. Parkland Memorial Hospital

247. John B. Connally

248. Arlington National Cemetery

249. Mary Jo Kopechne

250. Doris Kearns Goodwin

251. William Kennedy Smith (He was acquitted.)

252. *George*

253. Jean Kennedy Smith

254. Edward Kennedy

Politics in Ireland

255. Mary McAleese

256. John Hume (Hume is the leader of the Social Democratic and Labour Party, Northern Ireland's largest Catholic party.)

257. David Trimble (Trimble is the Ulster Unionist Party leader.)

258. Conor Cruise O'Brien

259. seven (Thomas J. Clarke, Sean MacDiarmada, Thomas MacDonagh, P. H. Pearse, Eamonn Ceannt, James Connolly, and Joseph Plunkett)

260. Stormont (outside Belfast)

261. Winston Churchill

262. the House of Representatives

263. both (The president is head of state only and does not have executive functions.)

264. Mary Robinson

265. All are dedicated to upholding and maintaining the constitution of Northern Ireland as an integral part of the United Kingdom.

266. Charles Haughey

267. the signing of the Anglo-Irish Agreement (The agreement gave the Republic of Ireland a say over Northern Ireland affairs.)

268. Garret Fitzgerald

269. the Irish Constitution (*Bunreacht Na hÉireann*)

270. Constance Gore-Booth (Countess Markiewicz)

271. Jim Larkin

CHAPTER FIVE.
The Irish Spin on Music

272. uilleann pipes

273. Bono

274. Boomtown Rats

275. Prince

276. goat

277. Derry

278. Bob Geldof

279. Josef Locke (Locke came out of his self-imposed exile in County Kildare to appear at the movie's premiere in London.)

280. Clannad

281. the Undertones (Upon their split in 1983, the O'Neill brothers went on to form That Petrol Emotion, while Feargal Sharkey went on to a solo career.)

282. Enya

283. Elvis Costello

284. Hothouse Flowers

285. John Field (1782–1837)

286. "Danny Boy," or "The Londonderry Air" (In 1910 F. E. Weatherly, an English lawyer, wrote the words and music for an unsuccessful song he called "Danny Boy." In 1912 his sister-in-law in America sent him a tune called "The Londonderry Air," which he had never heard before. He immediately noticed that the melody was perfectly fitted to his "Danny Boy" lyrics and published a revised version of the song in 1913.)

287. the Chieftains

288. *Amhrán Na bhFiann*

289. Patrick Sarsfield Gilmore (The song is attributed to Gilmore under his pseudonym, Louis Lambert. There is some controversy as to whether he actually composed the melody, as he was heard on several occasions to claim that it was a Negro spiritual he had simply adapted. Others contend that it was a traditional Irish air. No Irish air with that melody has ever come to light, however, so that theory may be just wishful thinking on the part of the Irish.)

290. Thomas Davis

Well-Known Irish Ballads

291. "Whiskey in the Jar"

292. "The Galway Shawl"

293. "Danny Boy"

294. "Carrickfergus"

295. "The Fields of Athenry"

296. "The Wild Rover"

297. "Slievenamon"

298. "Spancil Hill"

299. "The Boys from the County Armagh"

300. "Molly Malone/In Dublin's Fair City"

301. Bono of U2

302. Horslips (Horslips broke onto the music scene in the early 1970s.)

303. Stiff Little Fingers

304. Tommy Makem

305. Lisdoonvarna

306. "A uniform so simple in its style. . . ." (from "The Broad Black Brimmer")

307. Comhaltas Ceoltóirí Éireann (The English translation is roughly "A Gathering of Irish Musicians." The organization is often called CCÉ, or simply Comhaltas.)

308. Frank Patterson (The Tipperary-born singer has recorded with the London Symphony Orchestra, the Academy of St. Martin in the Fields, and the Royal Philharmonic Orchestra. He has also appeared with major orchestras in the United States and Europe.)

309. *Faith of Our Fathers*

310. the Chieftains (The legendary harpist's career includes a variety of musical achievements in both classical and folk music. He has made more than thirty recordings. Besides the harp, Bell is an accomplished musician on the oboe, horn, cor anglais, hammer dulcimer, and keyboards.)

311. Lead singer Boy George's real name is George O'Dowd, and his father is from County Tipperary.

312. Cherish the Ladies

313. "Too-ra-loo-ra-loo-ral (That's an Irish Lullaby)"

314. Derek Warfield

315. Belfast

316. James Galway (flautist)

317. Bing Crosby ("White Christmas," written by Irving Berlin for the 1942 film *Holiday Inn*, is Crosby's best-selling recording. It is also the best-selling Christmas single of all time, with over 30 million copies sold.)

318. John Francis McCormack (1884–1945) (At the end of World War I, he sang "The Battle Hymn of the Republic" and "The Star-Spangled Banner" before President Wilson at a ceremony by Washington's grave at Mount Vernon.)

319. *Finian's Rainbow*

320. Phil Lynott, bass guitar (Philip Lynott lost his battle with drugs and died of heart failure and pneumonia on January 4, 1986, at the age of thirty-five.)

321. the Irish Rovers

322. Slane Castle

323. Paul McCartney

324. the assassination of Martin Luther King Jr.

325. Van Morrison

326. Bill Whelan

327. Tommy Makem

328. Fiddler's Green Festival

329. Van Morrison

330. Elvis Presley (CBS censored the singer's hips so his gyrations wouldn't offend viewers.)

331. Sinead O'Connor

Who Recorded It?

332. Van Morrison

333. the Undertones

334. Thin Lizzy

335. Four Men & a Dog

336. U2

337. the Cranberries

338. Boyzone

339. Boomtown Rats

340. Horslips

341. Hothouse Flowers

CHAPTER SIX.
Irish on the Silver Screen

342. John Mills

343. Pierce Brosnan

344. Alfred Hitchcock (It was his second film.)

345. Maureen O'Sullivan (During a career that spanned more than sixty years, O'Sullivan, mother of actress Mia Farrow, appeared in over seventy-two films, television productions, and Broadway shows.)

346. Johnny Weissmuller

347. Parker

348. the Delorean motorcar (Deloreans were built in Dunmurry, close to Belfast.)

349. *Shake Hands with the Devil*

350. actor Stephen Boyd, who was born in Belfast (In the movie, Boyd played the part of the Roman tribune Messala. At the time of its release, the $15 million *Ben-Hur* was the most expensive film ever made.)

351. Aidan Quinn

352. *Legends of the Fall*

353. Ardmore Studios (Ardmore's credits include *The Lion in Winter, Excalibur,* and *My Left Foot.*)

354. *The Quiet Man*

355. He accidentally killed a man in the ring.

356. Trooper Thornton

357. Michaeleen Flynn

358. *Patriot Games*

359. Mickey Rourke

360. *A Prayer for the Dying*

361. Martin Fallon

362. *Miller's Crossing*

363. Roddy Doyle (The three books/films are *The Commitments, The Snapper,* and *The Van.*)

364. *The Snapper*

365. Wilson Pickett

366. John Ford (The movies are *The Informer* (1935), *The Grapes of Wrath* (1940), *How Green Was My Valley* (1941), and *The Quiet Man* (1952). Born Sean O'Feeny, Ford directed more than 130 movies. A statue in his hometown of Portland, Maine, celebrates his legacy.)

367. *The Plough and the Stars*

368. Spencer Tracy

369. rugby (The movie received two Academy Award nominations: Richard Harris for Best Actor and Rachel Roberts for Best Actress.)

370. Liam Neeson

371. *The Dead Pool*

372. *Leap of Faith*

373. *My Favorite Year*

374. *The Dead*

375. Danny LaRue

376. John Lynch

377. *Eat the Peach*

378. Donald O'Connor

379. Mickey Rooney

380. Daniel Day-Lewis

381. *My Left Foot* (Directed by Jim Sheridan, the movie received five Academy Award nominations.)

382. Ray McAnally

383. in a car crash

384. Kenneth Branagh

385. Milo O'Shea

Irish on the Small Screen

386. *All in the Family*

387. Ed McMahon

388. Roma Downey

389. Maureen O'Boyle

390. *Remington Steele*

391. Chief Engineer Miles O'Brien

392. *Omega 7*

393. CBS

394. *The Life of Riley*

395. Cunningham

396. Dermot Morgan

397. Ed O'Neill

398. Jackie Gleason

399. Walter Brennan

400. Senator Joseph McCarthy

401. Jacqueline Kennedy

402. Ed Sullivan

403. John McLaughlin (His TV show is *The McLaughlin Group.*)

404. Liam Neeson

405. Mickey Rooney

CHAPTER SEVEN.
Name That Film:
The Irish Connection

406. *In the Name of the Father*

407. Emma Thompson

408. *Far and Away*

409. Boston

410. *Michael Collins*

411. Detective Ned Broy

412. *The Devil's Own*

413. Frankie McGuire

414. *The Field*

415. one (Richard Harris for Best Actor)

416. *The Crying Game*

417. Forest Whitaker

418. *Hidden Agenda*

419. John Stalker

420. *Odd Man Out*

421. the Crown Bar

422. *Darby O'Gill and the Little People*

423. King Brian

424. *Hear My Song*

425. tax difficulties

426. *High Spirits*

427. Peter O'Toole

428. *Cal*

429. Pat O'Connor

430. *The Molly Maguires*

431. Richard Harris

432. *I Went Down*

433. Frank Grogan

434. *Belfast Assassin* (titled *Harry's Game* in Europe)

435. Clannad

436. *Some Mother's Son*

437. Helen Mirren and Fionnula Flanagan

438. *Eat the Peach*

439. *Roustabout*

440. *Song o' My Heart*

441. Frank Borzage

442. *Lamb*

443. Liam Neeson

444. *The Matchmaker*

445. Massachusetts

446. *Da*

447. Barnard Hughes

448. *Blown Away*

449. *The Dolphin*

450. *My Left Foot*

451. Brenda Fricker (Best Supporting Actress)

452. *Only the Lonely*

453. Danny Muldoon

454. *The Brothers McMullen* (directed by Edward Burns)

455. three

456. *No Surrender*

457. Elvis Costello

458. *The Playboys*

459. Albert Finney

460. *The Butcher Boy*

461. Patrick McCabe

462. *The Secret of Roan Inish*

463. Selkie

464. *Finian's Rainbow*

465. Francis Ford Coppola

466. *Into the West*

467. his producing debut (Byrne was the associate producer of the film.)

468. *Yankee Doodle Dandy* (Cohan's great, all-time classic show tunes include "You're a Grand Old Flag," "Give My Regards to Broadway," "Over There," and "Yankee Doodle Dandy.")

469. John Huston (His father was Walter Huston.)

CHAPTER EIGHT.
Telling the Tale: Irish Literature

470. *Ulysses* by James Joyce (Seventy-three years after it was first published, Joyce's *Ulysses* still sells one hundred thousand copies a year.)

471. *The Great Gatsby*

472. Francis

473. Liam O'Flaherty

474. *Gone With the Wind*

475. Pete Hamill

476. Seamus Heaney

477. George Bernard Shaw

478. *A Monk Swimming*

479. Roddy Doyle

480. Oscar Wilde

481. Gerry Adams, president of Sinn Fein

482. Oscar Wilde

483. Kate Chopin

484. Galway Kinnell

485. William Gibson

486. F. Scott Fitzgerald

487. four

488. William Butler Yeats (1923), George Bernard Shaw (1925), Samuel Beckett (1969), and Seamus Heaney (1995)

489. Eugene O'Neill

490. William Kennedy

491. *The Hostage*

492. b. A.D. 800

493. b. the four gospels

494. coal

495. *The Playboy of the Western World*

496. Lady Isabella Augusta Gregory

497. New Abbey Theatre

498. Margaret Mitchell

499. Thomas Moore

500. James Stephens

501. William Butler Yeats

502. Marcus Cook (Marc) Connelly

503. J. F. (James Farl) Powers

504. Joel Chandler Harris (Harris's father was an Irish laborer who deserted Harris's mother before the child was born.)

505. George Bernard Shaw (The play was *Pygmalion*.)

506. "the uneatable"

507. *Breakfast in Babylon*

508. Eugene O'Neill

509. W. B. Yeats

510. Lemuel

511. Walter Macken

512. George Bernard Shaw

513. Seamus Heaney

514. Mary Higgins Clark

515. W. B. Yeats

Irish Literary Figures and Their Works

516. Bram Stoker

517. Frank McCourt

518. John F. Kennedy

519. Eugene O'Neill

520. Pete Hamill

521. Roddy Doyle

522. Thomas Cahill

523. Seamus Heaney

524. Maeve Binchy

525. Margaret Mitchell

526. George Bernard Shaw

527. Flannery O'Connor

528. Oscar Wilde

529. Brendan Behan

530. Jonathan Swift

531. John M. Synge

532. F. Scott Fitzgerald

533. James Joyce

534. W. B. Yeats

535. Mary McCarthy

The Artist—James Joyce

536. *Dubliners*

537. Clongowes Wood College (run by the Jesuits)

538. *A Portrait of the Artist as a Young Man*

539. Paris

540. *Ulysses*

541. *Finnegans Wake*

542. Catholic Church

543. Daniel O'Connell

544. a perforated ulcer

CHAPTER NINE.

The Irish Take on Sports

545. Charles A. Comiskey (1858–1931)

546. John L. Sullivan

547. James J. Corbett (Sullivan won the last bare knuckles title bout over Jake Kilrain in 1889, but, using gloves under the new Queensberry rules, he lost to Corbett in 1892.)

548. *Gentleman Jim* (Errol Flynn portrayed Corbett in the movie.)

549. the Bronx

550. Jimmy Connors (winner) and John McEnroe (runner-up)

551. Barry McGuigan

552. Dennis Taylor

553. Pat Eddery

554. Maureen "Little Mo" Connolly

555. Stephen Roche (Besides winning the Tour de France, Roche also won the Tour of Italy in 1987 and picked up the title of world champion.)

556. Mount Clemens (When John L. Sullivan failed to visit Mount Clemens in 1892, before his celebrated match with Jim Corbett, the *Mount Clemens Monitor* lamented the fact that Sullivan had evidently forgotten that Mount Clemens was responsible for his successes and boldly predicted that the Great Bostonian was about to lose his title. The rest, as they say, is history!)

557. Steve Cruz (Inactive in 1987, McGuigan returned to the ring in April 1988. He had four fights, losing his last fight to Jim McDonnell in four rounds. He was defeated only three times in his professional career—by Cruz, McDonnell, and Peter Eubanks. He defeated Peter Eubanks in a return fight.)

558. Michelle Smith

559. 400-meter individual medley, 400-meter freestyle, 200-meter individual medley (Smith also won bronze in the 200-meter butterfly. In all she has won more gold medals for Ireland than anyone else in history.)

560. two

561. horse (The Irish Hunter, now known as the Irish Draught Sport Horse, was produced by crossing the Irish Draught with the Thoroughbred and is considered the best cross-country horse in the world.)

562. Croke Park, Dublin

563. Belgian Grand Prix (Jordan Grand Prix became the twenty-fifth team to be a race winner in the history of the FIA World Championship.)

Sports Stars—Past and Present

564. soccer

565. rugby

566. boxing

567. Formula One racing

568. athletics

569. boxing

570. athletics

571. show jumping

572. baseball

573. boxing

574. golf

575. rugby

576. steeplechase

577. soccer

578. boxing

579. Gaelic football

580. rowing

581. American football

582. athletics

583. a. the Curragh

584. c. a fake hare

585. a. the Derby

586. b. 300 (approximately)

587. c. 1989

588. b. rugby

589. c. Michael Carruth

590. c. marathon

591. b. Tour of Spain

592. lightweight coxless four (rowing)

593. Eddie Irvine

594. hurling

595. James Brendan Connolly, who won triple jump gold at the Athens Olympics in 1896 (He also won silver in the high jump and bronze in the long jump that year. The first gold medal winner of the modern Olympic Games did not get permission from Harvard University to travel to Athens. Upon his return, he was barred from further study. In 1949 Harvard awarded the by-then eighty-one-year-old writer an honorary degree.)

596. greyhound (The dog, a feeble-looking runt of a Waterford litter, was saved from drowning by a little boy. Trained in Lurgan, County Armagh, the dog was memorialized in poetry and song for astounding British dog purists by winning the Waterloo Cup in 1869.)

597. Christy Roche

598. mountaineering (He was the first Irishman to climb the 26,401-foot-high Broad Peak in the Himalayas.)

599. Larry Bird

600. Larry Bird, Kevin McHale, and Robert Parish

601. *Celtic Pride*

602. William Harrison "Jack" Dempsey (It is believed that Jess Willard, in losing his heavyweight title to Dempsey in 1919, received one of the greatest beatings any fighter has ever suffered. He retired at the end of the third round with a broken jaw, two broken ribs, a closed eye, and a partial loss of hearing.)

603. "Iron Mike"

604. Gene Tunney

605. Dempsey did not go to a neutral corner immediately. (The referee delayed the count until Dempsey went to a neutral corner. Tunney got up at the count of nine and went on to win the bout on a decision. The count of nine was estimated to be a count of fourteen!)

606. Mickey Cochrane

607. amateur athletics

608. Gaelic Athletic Association (GAA)

609. Irish Derby

610. Michael Joseph "King" Kelly

611. They all became members of the National Baseball Hall of Fame.

612. Charles "Kid" McCoy (It is also believed that the term "the Real McCoy" was coined because of him. To gain a psychological advantage over his opponents, McCoy often pretended to be ill or out of shape. On fight night McCoy was usually fit and ready to fight, leading people to wonder, "Is this the real McCoy?")

613. chess (He was the first, though unofficial, world chess champion. In an interview, international grandmaster Bobby Fischer commented on Morphy, saying, "Morphy . . . I think everyone agrees . . . was probably the greatest of them all.")

614. He became the first Rangers player to have his number (34) retired.

615. billiards (Phelan, the owner of a New York billiard parlor, published a book, *Billiards Without Masters*, that went through ten editions between 1850 and 1875. As a manufacturer, Phelan is credited with adding the diamond markers to billiard tables to assist in aiming, particularly on bank shots.)

616. Frank Leahy

617. George Best

618. hurling (The award goes to the winner of the All-Ireland Championship.)

619. c. 1986

620. Ray Houghton (Ireland, heavy underdogs in the contest, won the game 1–0.)

621. tennis

622. Walter O'Malley (He also blacked out television broadcasts of home games, a move that many claim has led

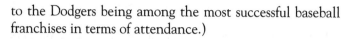

to the Dodgers being among the most successful baseball franchises in terms of attendance.)

623. Wayne McCullough

624. Jack Dempsey

625. They are all winners of the Irish Derby (horse race).

626. Kildare

627. Mark McGwire (McGwire shattered Roger Maris's record for home runs in a season by hitting seventy homers in 1998.)

628. Shergar (Shergar went down in racing history for having the largest margin of victory ever at the English Derby. The white-faced bay finished ten lengths ahead in 1981 and went on to take the Irish Derby and King George VI and Queen Elizabeth Stakes at Ascot.)

CHAPTER TEN. The Fighting Irish: Irish in the Military

629. Andrew Jackson

630. "Garryowen" (It also became the official tune of the First Cavalry Division in 1981.)

631. Robert McNamara, secretary of the Department of Defense

632. the "Irish Brigade"

633. Illinois (Twenty-third Illinois Volunteers, also known as the "Illinois Irish Brigade")

634. Notre Dame University

635. Battalion de San Patricio

636. Major General William "Wild Bill" Donovan

637. He is the only American to have received the nation's four highest awards, the Medal of Honor, the Distinguished Service Cross, the Distinguished Service Medal, and the National Security Medal.

638. General Patrick Cleburne (Cleburne was also one of two foreign-born officers to attain the rank of major general in the Confederate armed forces.)

639. *PT-109*

640. Commodore John Barry (In the space of fifty-eight years, the son of a poor Irish tenant farmer rose from humble cabin boy to senior commander of the entire U.S. fleet.)

641. SS *Jeremiah O'Brien* (The *Jeremiah O'Brien*'s engine room was used to film the engine room scenes in the movie *Titanic.*)

642. It returned to Normandy to take part in the fiftieth anniversary of D-Day. (It is the only ship left of the Allied armada—some 5,500 ships strong—that stormed the Normandy beaches on D-Day. The vessel is also one of two fully restored operating survivors of 2,710 World War II liberty ships.)

643. Lieutenant Commander Edward Henry ("Butch") O'Hare of the U.S. Navy (O'Hare was the son of Edward J. O'Hare, wheeler-dealer millionaire lawyer, federal informant, and partner in crime of Al Capone's.)

644. "Fighting" Father Duffy (Duffy was born in Canada of Irish immigrant parents. Today, a monument to Duffy stands in Times Square.)

645. Davy Crockett

646. Charles Carroll III

647. a. 200

648. c. 160,000 (Actually, there were a little more than 160,000 Irish-born soldiers in the Union army.)

649. Roger Casement

650. He was the founder and leader of the St. Patrick's Battalion (Battalion de San Patricios).

651. Patrick Sarsfield

652. Colonel Michael Corcoran

653. Bull Run

654. a harp

655. Brian Boru (It is said that the battle was so fierce that in places the trees wept blood and the nearby River Tolka turned red. Boru was actually too old to participate in the battle and was reportedly slain by the Vikings in his tent.)

656. Joseph (Joe Jr. was posthumously awarded the Navy Cross and the Air Medal and had a destroyer—the USS *Joseph P. Kennedy, Jr.*—dedicated to him as a tribute to a gallant officer and his heroic devotion to duty.)

657. Bridget Divers

658. Sullivan (The "Fighting Sullivan Brothers" became national heroes. Later, Congress passed the "Sullivan law," which would prevent brothers from serving on the same ship.)

659. Bartlett Laffey

660. Thomas Meagher

661. photography (The Civil War was the first to be fully documented by the fledgling art of photography. Matthew Brady was among the most famous of the Civil War photographers, having convinced Abraham Lincoln to let him photograph the Union army in camp and in battle.)

662. Canada (In April 1866 John O'Mahoney, founder of the Fenian Brotherhood, attempted to capture Campo Bello off the New Brunswick coast; this was followed by the May battle on the Canadian shore when eight hundred Fenians took Fort Eire.)

663. William Joyce, also known as "Lord Haw-Haw" (Joyce obtained a British passport in 1938, an event that would lead to his trial and subsequent hanging for treason in 1945.)

664. William Brown

665. Don Bernardo O'Higgins (1778–1842)

666. Maryland

667. Major Thomas Buchanan McGuire Jr. (of the United States Army Air Corps)

668. Boston (The British built Castle William during the Revolutionary War, and it is said that George Washington ordered his troops, when approaching Dorchester Heights on March 17, 1776, to use the password "St. Patrick" just the day before the British evacuated Boston.)

669. Medal of Honor

670. Audie Murphy

671. *To Hell and Back*

672. Clan Na Gael

673. shamrocks

CHAPTER ELEVEN. Irish Stew: General Irish Knowledge

674. Éire

675. Hibernia

676. the Free State (1921), Éire (1937), and the Republic of Ireland (1949)

677. It is a fossil fuel that is similar to coal but usually dark brown in color. (It is estimated that Ireland has 1 billion tons of lignite in reserves.)

678. pig (Pigs are the most common farm animal in Ireland.)

679. Sinn Féin

680. the Irish economy (One of the poorest in the European Union during the 1980s, the Republic of Ireland's economy grew rapidly in the 1990s, echoing the "tiger" economies of East Asia.)

681. the currency of the Republic of Ireland

682. b. 20 percent

683. b. 70 million

684. Omagh, County Tyrone

685. She became the first Catholic woman to be ordained a priest in either Ireland or Britain.

686. Michael Collins

687. China

688. Europa Hotel

689. Giant's Causeway

690. the island of Ireland (these being the southernmost and northernmost points of the island)

691. Nobel Prize in physics (for his pioneer work in transmutation of atomic nuclei)

692. c. 470,000 (Approximately one-third of all visitors to Northern Ireland that year were from the Republic of Ireland.)

Irish—It's in the Name

693. Irish coffee

694. Irish linen

695. Irish stew

696. Irish yew

697. Irish terrier

698. Irish elk

699. Irish bull

700. Irish moss

701. Irish lord

702. Irish tweed

703. turf (peat)

704. Claddagh ring

705. the crown

706. Galway

707. Blarney Castle

708. Kerry

709. Aran sweater

710. Ballycastle, County Antrim

711. two (*Olympic* and *Brittannic* were also built in Belfast. The *Titanic* was the second of three large liners intended to work the Southampton–New York "shuttle" service. The sister ships were planned to be near identical.)

712. Garda Siochana

713. It has two Nobel Prize winners among its alumni. (Seamus Heaney won the Nobel Prize in literature in 1995, and John Hume won the Nobel Peace Prize in 1998.)

714. Valencia Island (The footprints are 385 million years old.)

715. Garth Brooks

716. Irish linen

717. May and June (averaging five to seven hours of sunshine per day)

718. Gulf Stream (or Gulf System)

719. Cardinal Cahal Daly (*Steps on My Pilgrim Journey: Memories and Reflections* recalls his time as archbishop and his thoughts on the many changes that have taken place in the Catholic Church over the past thirty years.)

720. Church of Ireland (The total membership of the Church of Ireland is around 380,000, 75 percent of whom live in Northern Ireland.)

721. b. 4 million (There are approximately 1,300 parishes served by about 4,000 priests.)

722. none (There are no snakes in Ireland, and the only reptile is the common lizard.)

723. c. 85 percent

724. Newgrange (Older than Stonehenge, this giant megalithic tomb was probably erected about 3,200 B.C. Its purpose is still relatively unknown, although it is most associated in Irish mythology with the god Aonghus.)

725. Dublin (The Gaelic is *Baile Átha Cliath.*)

726. Environmental Protection Agency

727. limestone

728. Dingle, County Kerry

729. the pneumatic tire

730. Mummers

Irish Food and Drink

731. distillation (The process was originally used for making perfume, but the Irish monks found a better use for it—they invented whiskey!)

732. c. 2,000

733. bacon and cabbage

734. b. 400

735. sausage (pork)

736. pot still

737. baking

738. Bushmills

739. Murphy's and Beamish

740. lamb or mutton

741. potatoes (also known as "potato griddle cakes")

742. spring onions (scallions)

743. Bailey's Irish Cream liqueur (The Dublin pub is the Bailey.)

744. Jameson

745. chopped kale or white cabbage

746. Galway (The famous mollusks are sampled by the ton during the festival, and many local restaurants and pubs have special menus and tastings.)

747. Kellogg's Corn Flakes

748. honey

749. lobster

750. Dulse is edible purple seaweed, while yellow man is a type of honeycombed toffee.